IMAGES OF WALES

PONTYPRIDD
REVISITED

IMAGES OF WALES

PONTYPRIDD
REVISITED

DEAN POWELL

TEMPUS

Frontispiece: Taliesin James (1856-1938), *c.* 1920. The professional harpist was one of five children born to Celia and James James. His father composed the melody of the Welsh National Anthem, Hen Wlad Fy Nhadau. Born in the same year of the composition, Taliesin later became a lecturer at the Welsh College of Music and Drama and played the harp at the unveiling ceremony of a statue designed by Sir William Goscombe John in memory of his father and grandfather Evan James (who wrote the lyrics). The event took place at Ynysangharad War Memorial Park on 23 July 1930 before an audience of more than 10,000 people.

First published 2007

Tempus Publishing
Cirencester Road, Chalford,
Stroud, Gloucestershire, GL6 8PE
www.tempus-publishing.com

Tempus Publishing is an imprint of NPI Media Group

British Library Cataloguing in Publication Data.
A catalogue record for this book is available from the British Library.

ISBN 978 0 7524 4376 8

Typesetting and origination by NPI Media Group
Printed in Great Britain

Introduction

Many people wrongly believe that Pontypridd developed within a few short years of the creation of its landmark bridge across the river Taff. However, in truth this frontier town was born out of the industrialisation of its surrounding valleys and transformed from a sleepy agricultural region into one of the largest in Wales. Its growth was due to three hugely important factors; firstly its proximity to the Glamorganshire Canal, allowing an easy route between industrial Merthyr and Cardiff; secondly the coming of the Taff Vale Railway, this time linking the docklands to the rapidly expanding Welsh coal field in the Rhondda and finally the combination of these two factors provided the ideal setting for the first major industralisation of the area with the coming of the Brown, Lenox & Co. Ltd chain works. Together they gave Pontypridd the foundations to develop into a major market town which blossomed at the very heart of industrial South Wales.

We cannot ignore the fact that the building of a magnificent bridge in 1756 by local stonemason William Edwards did indeed give this area a form of identity. On his third attempt he succeeded in his aim to allow farmers easy access over the Taff by creating an architectural splendour, portrayed by a variety of artists who flocked there to gaze on his splendid achievement, nothing less than the longest single-arch bridge in the world. Although it did little to change the rural character of the district, the bridge led to the growth of a small cluster of houses on either side of the Taff and the area was named Newbridge – which makes us believe that there were probably several wooden old bridges along this stretch of the river. It was another century before the town was renamed Pontypridd.

By the end of the eighteenth century the first phase of industrialisation in Newbridge were under way. The most significant event was the opening of the Glamorganshire Canal in 1794. In the next three-and-a-half years workmen sliced through a 25-mile channel and the canal became a vital component that turned Newbridge into a major municipal centre. By 1818 a large chainworks was opened, marking the first example of industry to come to the area since the opening of the tinplate works in neighbouring Treforest.

The next phase of industrialisation began with the Taff Vale Railway in 1840 which, like the canal, ran from Merthyr to Cardiff. No one had anticipated the enormous growth of the Rhondda coal industry which would follow the opening of a level at Gyfeillion, a mile from Newbridge, by Dr Richard Griffiths in 1790 and of another by Walter Coffin at Dinas in 1807. Turning the lush green Rhondda into something of a vast black Klondyke, those early mining pioneers penetrated indiscriminately into the valley floor for their precious black gold. It was an event which had a tremendous effect on Newbridge as the town found that it was ideally placed for transporting coal to the docks. As the region produced most of the coal and iron on which the economy of the British Empire depended, the peak of production in 1913 saw 57-million tons of steam coal pass through the town to Barry and Cardiff. Pontypridd had the longest railway platform in Britain in an effort to cope with its 500 trains and 11,000 passengers per day.

The pace and extent of the growth of the town in late Victorian and early Edwardian times was breathtaking. By 1839, Newbridge had acquired a police force and in 1850 it had lighting in the main streets. A county court met in 1851 and it had 1,000 homes and thirty-three public houses. In 1856 the first post office opened and the town changed its name to Pontypridd, largely due to a decision by the local postmaster. During the same year a father and son who worked a local woollen factory had a profound effect on the musical history of Wales. Evan James and his son James penned a haunting Welsh hymn which was eventually named Hen Wlad Fy Nhadau and became the National Anthem of their homeland.

During the twilight years of Victoria's reign Pontypridd's status as a major market town and urban area was strengthened. Following the widespread growth of Nonconformism and the building of many chapels, St Catherine's church was built in 1869, complete with its domineering spire overlooking the bustling town. The first newspaper was established in 1873, and by 1885 there was a horse-drawn tram service, closely followed by the electric tram and trolleybus. A new town hall was built in 1890 and a public library opened its doors. In 1905 the municipal building was opened for Pontypridd Urban District Council and in the middle of the town a charming fountain was erected. The town played host to the National Eisteddfod of 1893 and established its own county school in 1896. Pontypidd's population had grown from 2,200 in 1847, to a staggering 38,000 in 1899.

With the passing of the First World War, Pontypridd folk dug deep in an effort to pay their respects to those who gave the ultimate sacrifice for freedom. No better monument could have been erected in their honour than with the opening of Ynysangharad War Memorial Park in 1923, the jewel in Pontypridd's crown. Culturally the town continued to blossom, particularly in the fields of choral singing and opera. In the sporting world Pontypridd produced world-famous boxers, cricketers, swimmers and of course its incredibly popular rugby team which was formed way back in the late 1870s.

Sadly, today Pontypridd bears the scars of deterioration, leaving this proud market town a different Pontypridd from its heyday in the Victorian era. Yet despite the many changes, seen all the more clearly when examining many of the photographs in this collection, our beloved 'Ponty' remains a unique town and one we hold so very dear to our hearts.

Dean Powell

2007

Pontypridd, *c.* 1860. Author Dean Powell was born in Llantrisant and is both a freeman and trustee of the town. He graduated from the University of Wales College of Swansea with a BA degree in English and Welsh. He became editor of the *Pontypridd & Llantrisant Observer* and literary editor of the *Western Mail* before becoming a broadcast journalist with BBC Radio Wales and news editor of GTFM Radio. He is currently a media liaison officer in local government and makes frequent appearances on TV and radio as a guest speaker. A member of Treorchy Male Choir for eighteen years, he is their regular compere and tenor soloist and has undertaken a series of successful tours to Canada, America and Australia where he performed in venues throughout Perth, Brisbane, Melbourne and at the Sydney Opera House. Dean is also their publicity officer and honorary archivist. This is his seventh book for Tempus and is dedicated with much love and gratitude to Colwyn Hill, for always being there.

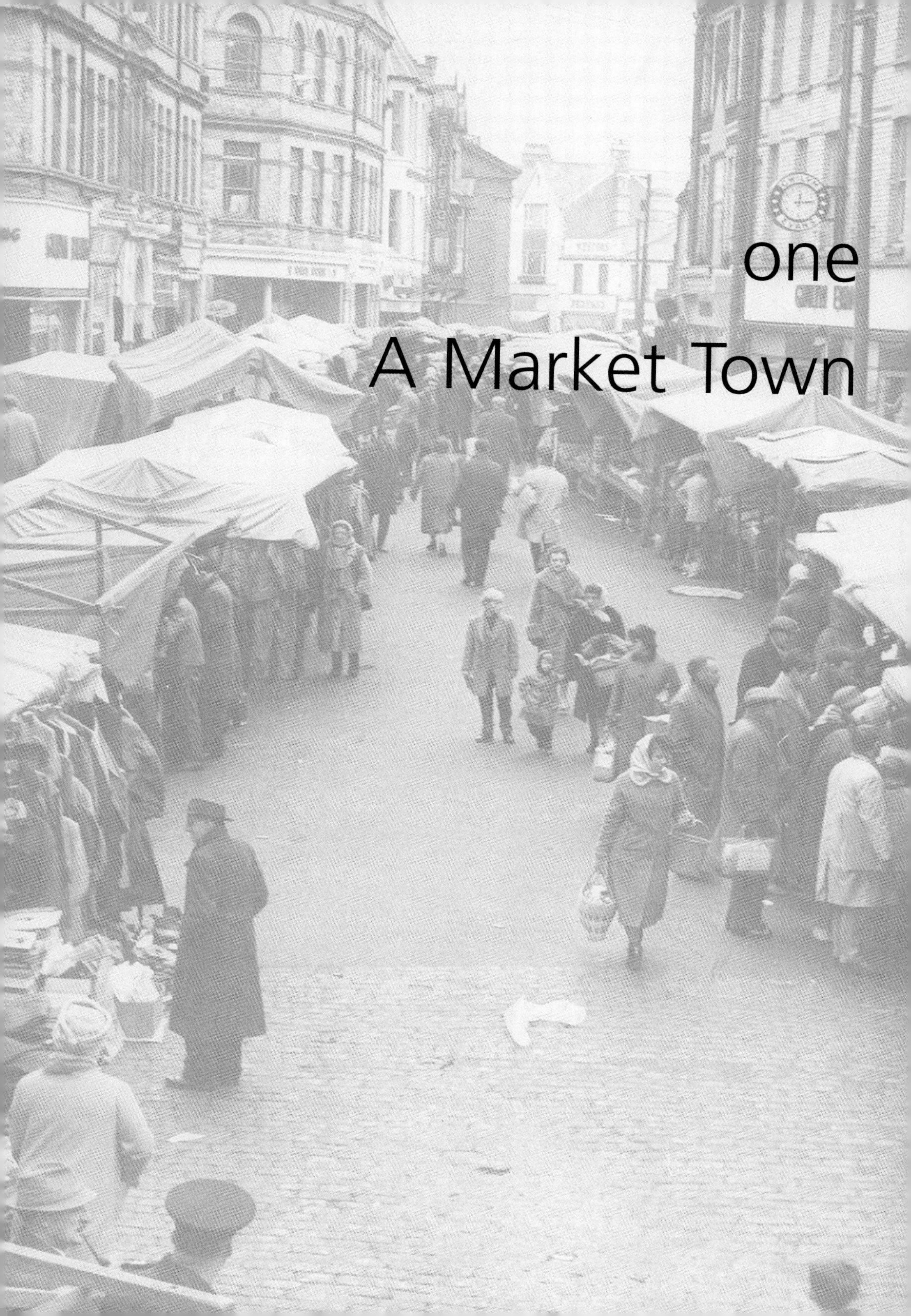

one

A Market Town

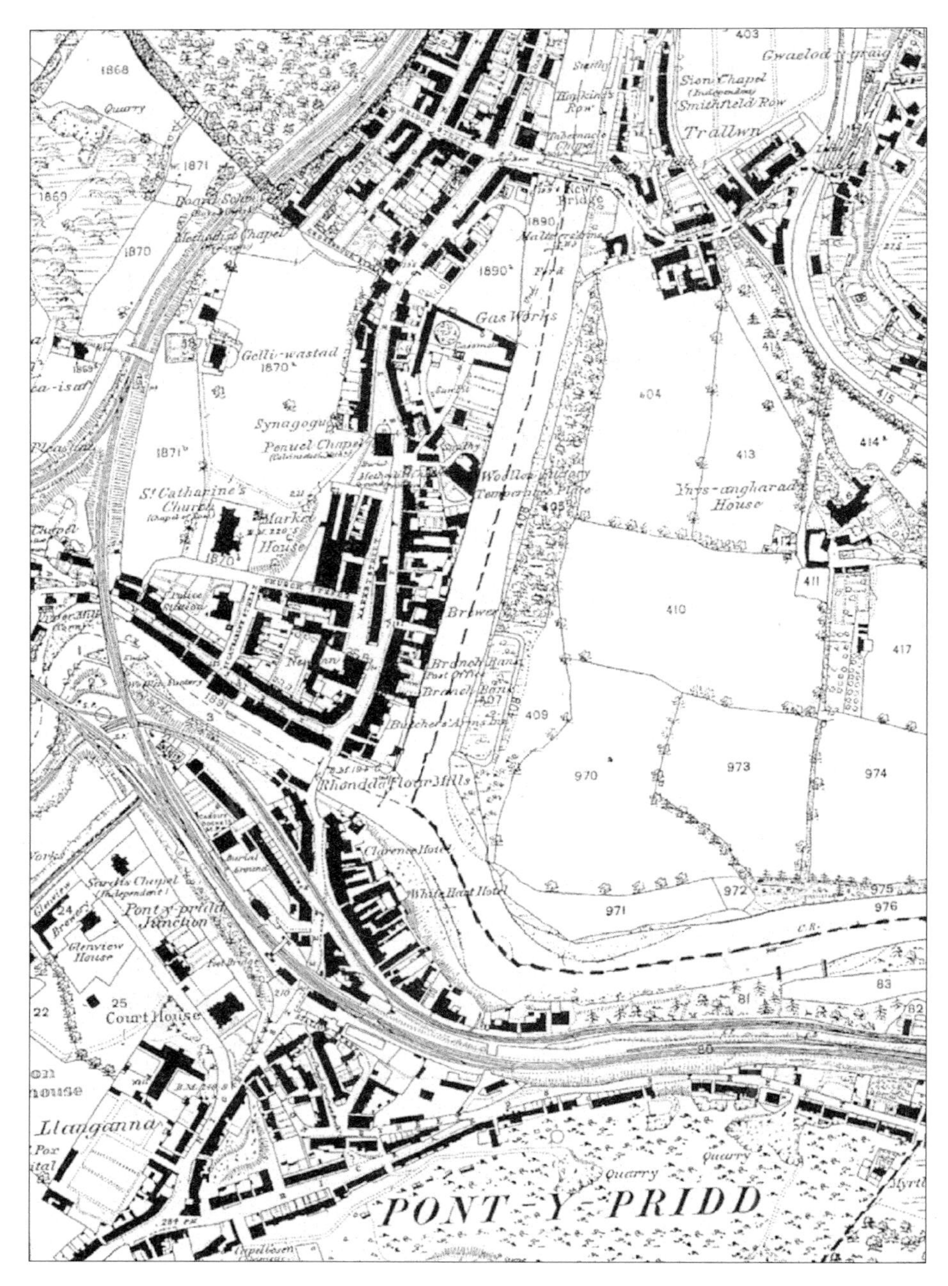

An Ordnance Survey map of Pontypridd in 1875. It is often assumed that Pontypridd's history began with the building of William Edwards's bridge across the river Taff in 1756. However, although the bridge attracted many visitors, it had little to offer in its immediate surroundings, unlike neighbouring Treforest which had fast become something of a bustling industrial area with the opening of the Tinplate works. It wasn't until the opening of the Glamorganshire Canal in 1794 and Newbridge Chain Works of Brown & Lenox in 1818 along with the growth of the mining industry in the Rhondda that the character of the district witnessed such significant development.

'A View near Newbridge' by Henry G. Gastineau (1791-1876), engraved by R. Roberts in 1830. The original name for Pontypridd was Newbridge and implies that there was an older, possibly wooden bridge crossing the river Taff prior to William Edwards's project. In John Leland's *Itinerary* (1536-42) listing bridges over the river Taff, he refers to a wooden bridge at Pont Rhehesk (Craig-yr-Hesg), a short distance upstream from Edwards Bridge. Reasons for the siting of that bridge may well have been for the use by pilgrims travelling to St Mary's Monastery at Penrhys. When Henry VIII closed the monastery in 1538 the local population would have had no need for a bridge, which would have fallen into decay. It would be more than 200 years before the need for a crossing would encourage the building of another bridge.

This drawing by I. Hafsell and engraved by I.C. Varrall called 'Ponty Pryd, Glamorganshire' depicts the area in 1818 – the year in which Brown Lenox opened their famous chainworks on the banks of the Glamorganshire Canal. The artist drew this view from the west bank of the Rhondda, William Edwards' bridge is in the background and Gelli Wastad House, owned by the Griffiths Family (builders of the Machine Bridge and Doctor's Canal in Treforest) can be seen on the left. The New Inn, home of Thomas Williams (Gwilym Morgannwg) is on the right.

A painting of William Edward's bridge, named 'Tour through the Vales of Glamorgan' by Thomas Hornoir in 1819. When local farmers despaired at being unable to cross the River Taff, except when the water level was low enough to use a ford, they commissioned William Edwards to build a bridge for £500. His first attempt was a three-arch structure, built in 1746 and sited slightly downstream from the present bridge. After two-and-a-half years, while William watched anxiously, tree trunks and other debris battered the bridge during a severe flood and it collapsed and washed away. He had pledged to maintain the bridge for seven years and had to reconstruct it. He conceived the idea of a one-arch bridge, the perfect segment of circle, 35ft high with a 140 ft chord or span, and a diameter of 175ft. Wheelwright Thomas Williams built a substantial centering to support the arch while it was under construction. Stone for the bridge was quarried locally. But when the bridge was nearing completion in 1751, it collapsed.

Old Bridge and Victoria Bridge from Zion Street. Following his two failed attempts, Edwards was in debt and discouraged, but a subscription of £700 promoted by Lord Talbot and Lord Windsor enabled him to finish the bridge. Until then he did not know the laws of equilibrium or balance, and the pressure caused by the 32 ft long by 20 ft high abutments, or haunches, of the bridge was so great that after several years the crown of the arch was forced upwards and the central section collapsed. Undaunted, he lightened the weight of the haunches by making three cylindrical openings of 3ft, 6ft and 9ft in diameter in each. The danger that the light curve of the bridge would spring upwards again was avoided. The Old Bridge was started in 1755 and completed in 1756, and was for many years one of the longest single-span bridges in the world.

Opening of the Victoria Bridge, 4 December 1857. A century after William Edward's bridge was built, the need for a second bridge was greater than ever. The original bridge could not cope with streams of carts and carriages that could barely pass each other. Solicitor Edward Colnett Spickett received letters for the new bridge to be built by Glamorgan Quarter Sessions and public subscription. Robert Hughes was the architect and the entire project cost £1,575. Stone was quarried from Trallwn and the bridge was built by Thomas Jenkins. It was opened by Revd George Thomas of Ystrad Mynach who contributed £500 towards it.

The original seventeenth-century Maltsers Pub which was built on the site of a small pub named the White Horse Inn. In 1808 Baptists met in the attic of the pub to hold their services until Carmel chapel was built in 1810. The pub was famous for its ghost in the cellar. One night a maid went down with a jug of ale and saw the misty figure of a man among the barrels. The spirit was apparently that of a bankrupt gambler who lost his money at cock-fighting bouts and told the girl he would only be set free if she went to the wooded valley of Cwm Pistyll Goleu at Llanwonno and found a set of 2 in spurs in a secret place near the waterfall. Legend has it that if she threw them in the River Taff he would find eternal rest.

Pontypridd, 1900. It was the village of Treforest rather than Pontypridd that experienced the preliminary phase of industrialisation. By the end of the nineteenth century a tinworks and small ironworks were in operation there. Treforest was also the terminus of a tram road constructed by Dr Richard Griffiths that ran from the first coalmines being sunk in the lower Rhondda. Dr Griffiths of Gelli Wastad House also built a private canal known as the Doctor's Canal that linked the tram road and the Glamorganshire Canal. Significantly, both the Doctor's Canal and tram road effectively ignored the tiny hamlet scattered around Edwards's bridge.

The long-since demolished cottages on the riverside of Berw Road and the rear of Tabernacle chapel, *c.* 1899. The pace and extent of the growth of Pontypridd in late Victorian and early Edwardian times was breathtaking. Population had grown from 2,200 in 1847, to 15,000 in 1861, to 20,000 in 1891 and to some 38,000 in 1899.

Bridge Street junction, *c.* 1960. The Bridge Inn was on Berw Road, and stands on what is now the site of the new police station. Nearby was the Ruperra Hotel, known for its boxing enthusiasts. In 1890s police visited the Bridge to question why the landlord was illegally serving drinks after hours. As the sergeant wrote intently, the bar emptied as the drinkers felt a need to go out the back. Their 'great escape' was discovered when a drunk fell into the gutter and started singing 'Sospan Fach'. The pub closed in July 1968 when the last landlord was Tom Evans.

E. Gould & Son on the corner of Bridge Street and the north end of Taff Street. The store specialised in sports gear of all types.

The north end of Taff Street, *c.* 1960. The tower-shaped building in the background was once a toll house leading to the cattle market. Robert Smyth, opened 'chemist, wines and spirits' there in April 1889. The tower was built on the corner of Turnpike Lane (also known as River Street and Ford Street) leading to the former cattle market. It later became Crosswell's Wine Shop and Off-Licence. The building, along with its neighbouring Tredeger Arms, Peglers and Garfields were all demolished when the Taff Vale Shopping Centre was opened in the mid-1960s.

The stables owned by Captain William Williams, *c.* 1890. The building was later demolished to make way for the YMCA. Captain Williams was a local brewer who owned the field known as Fairfield opposite his home leading to the river Taff. It is now occupied as part of the car park and Taff Vale Shopping Precinct.

Taff Street with the YMCA on the left. Taff Street emerged as the town's main marketing street and all other identified streets on the 1841 census were also located on the western side of the River Taff including High Street, Mill Street, Crossbank Street, Market Street and Bridge Street. Development was also seen in Trallwn, Ynysangharad and Coedpenmaen on the eastern side.

Danygraig House was situated at No. 28 Taff Street. This nineteenth- century building was owned by William Williams' family and was later the home of the YMCA opened by Sir Clifford Cory MP on 29 September 1910. The YMCA was created in a bid to occupy the free time of young men. Sports and other social activities were organised on a regular basis to offer them an alternative to crime and alcohol. During the same year the Pontypridd Labour Exchange was also opened in the town.

Demolishing Bridge Street as part of the planned redevelopment of the north end of the town, December 1963. It saw the end of such premises as Marenghis, Old Bridge Café and Old Bridge Pharmacy.

Above: The corner of Taff and Bridge Street prior to the demolishing of many of these properties to make way for the Taff Vale Shopping Centre.

Below: Taff Vale Shopping Centre, *c.* 1970. Within less than twenty years the 'modern', concrete shopping centre had become a major eyesore for the market town.

Above: A view of Lanwood including Tyfica Road, 1964. Pictured are various schools in this area of the town including Coedylan Secondary Modern and Pontypridd Boys' Grammar School. Also notice the railway sidings below and the original Pontypridd District Club. Coedylan School has since been demolished and the pupils and staff transferred to one site opened on the former Albion Colliery land in neighbouring Cilfynydd.

Below: Penuel Square, *c.*1955. To the right can be seen Pontypridd General Stores, Fey's Fountain record store and jewellers, S. Stone with an optician's shop above.

A view of Taff Street, *c.* 1980. Notice the concrete façade which totally obliterated the original frontage of the New Town Hall. To the left of this picture once stood Berlin House (No. 52 Taff Street) where E.M. Kuner sold a wide range of fancy goods during the 1890s such as shopping baskets, fender stools, dolls and silks.

General view of Pontypridd. In 1965 Pontypridd was twinned with the historic German town of Nurtingen near Stuttgart. The twinning was established by Cor Meibion Pontypridd who formed a link with the Oberensingen Male Choir in the town and so a formal agreement was signed by John Cheesman JP, mayor of Pontypridd and Karl Gonser, mayor of Nurtingen in July 1968. Since then there have been many successful exchange visits between schools, musical and sporting organisations.

Penuel chapel, *c.* 1964. Penuel Calvinistic Methodist chapel and the square was a familiar area for temperance speakers to address the crowds over the years. Cambrian Lane, a market entrance roadway running beside Penuel chapel, was known as Occupation Road. It was an appropriate name as many craftsmen worked there from the 1840s in the little cottages and workshops and in the bordering area where the New Town Hall was later built.

Probably the most familiar of market salesmen in Pontypridd was cockle-seller Tom Marshman. Known affectionately as 'Old Tom Cockles', he began selling cockles in the district when he was just fourteen, obtaining his supplies from relatives in Kidwelly. His horse and cart, and cries of 'Cockles Kidwelly, good for the belly' were part and parcel of the culture of the Graig, where he lived for most of his life. Tom had a wooden leg, and the tale goes that if he rode with his leg inside the cart it was going to rain. However if it hung outside the cart as he travelled along it was a sure sign of fine weather to come!

Above: Fraternal Parade following the demolition of Penuel chapel. Another major planning disaster, it saw the loss of a great landmark building in Pontypridd town centre. To the right of the Fountain is Hurleys record and toy shop, run by sisters Vera and Evelyn.

Left: The Fountain, *c.* 1890. Canopied with Celtic interlace and inscriptions, the four drinking bowls were designed by C.B. Fowler. The stone drinking fountain was unveiled in 1895 by its donor Sir Alfred Thomas, MP for East Glamorgan, (later Lord Pontypridd). It was designed to provide fresh drinking water to passers-by and animals. The relief inscriptions on the undersides of the projecting bowls reads: Duw a Digon/Heb Dduw Heb Ddim (God is Everything/Without God Without Anything).

Opposite above: Fred Fey Record Shop, *c.* 1960. A familiar haunt of young Tom Woodward (later Tom Jones), he used to make almost daily visits to the shop to listen to his favourite singers such as Jerry Lee Lewis. For more than a decade one of the counter girls was young Carole Hooper – the author's mother.

Below: Fred Fey (1902-1966) and Pat Miller behind the counter at the Fountain record shop. Mr Fey was born in Bristol, attending the same school as Hollywood star Cary Grant. He left school to concentrate on his work as a piano tuner, eventually moving to Cardiff to take up a post in Heath's Piano Co. in the city. Following the Second World War he opened his own piano repair and refurbishment business in a small shop in Penuel Lane before eventually renting a shop on the Fountain for his repair work. He later expanded the business to include selling sheet music and when his daughter Jean left school in the early 1950s to work in the shop, was encouraged to start selling records as well. It developed into one of the most popular stores in Pontypridd before eventually closing in the 1960s when the record business was sold to the shop next door, Hurley's Toys.

ALEXANDRE
OLIVER'S

HOSKINS
TRITSCHLER
FOR
SPECTACLES
MAKER OF
Mr E. HOSKINS
Artificial Teeth
HOSKINS
FOR
HOSKINS
THE NOTED WATCHMAKER
TRITSCHLER
CONSULT
FOR TEETH
TRITSCHLER'S

Taff Street around 1965, pictured just a short time before Penuel chapel on the right was demolished for the Fraternal Parade of shops to be built.

Right: The staff of Star Supply Stores, Taff Street, 1923.

Opposite above: Taff and Market Street, *c.* 1955. One of the most comical episodes in the history of the town occurred during the Taff Vale railway strike of 1900 when Thomas & Evans of Porth occupied a shop on the Fountain. Known as the manufacturers of Corona pop they used a large steam-driven traction engine to haul cartloads of drinks to Pontypridd but the vibration on Taff Street caused shopkeepers to complain to the UDC. It was proposed they be banned from using this method of transportation because it shook bottles on chemists' shelves violently. But no action was taken after one councillor said, 'Chemists have no reason to complain because they keep telling us their medicines should be shaken before taken'!

Opposite below: Hoskins and T. Evans decorators store on Taff Street, 1905. Hoskins advertised itself as the 'Maker of Artificial Teeth'. In the centre is Mr Wiggins, the dental mechanic who later set up his own business after the war and to the right is Mr Hoskins, the owner of the store.

Above: W. Oswal Davies, chemist. The owner was the first child enrolled in the new Pontypridd Boys' Grammar School. The shop was previously owned by chemist and seedsman Oliver Davies.

Below: Cambrian Temperance Hotel on the corner of Market Street and Cambrian Lane. The need for a temperance hotel was hardly unfounded as Pontypridd had up to 100 pubs during the last quarter of the nineteenth century. Some were simple beer houses which served ale in the parlour, others were rebuilt, altered and had their names changed. In the late Victorian era, those who were deemed drunk and disorderly received fines of 5s or 10s.

Taff Street featuring the ever-popular café and restaurant, The Prince's, *c.*1968.

Market Street, *c.* 1895. The growth of Pontypridd's famous market can be measured by its entry in *Pigott's Directory* of 1835 which illustrates that the market was larger than that neighbouring Treforest.

Pontypridd Market's fish and poultry stall owned by J. Robotham and E. Fellowes, 1939.

Market Street, *c.* 1900. Many of the brakes and cabs were made in Morgan Street by the Pontypridd Coach building & Wheelwright Co.

Market Street, *c.* 1920. There has been a market in Pontypridd since 1805, mainly for country folk to sell and barter their wares. In 1860 a new market, at first in its own hall but soon spilling out into the streets, began attracting shoppers from far and wide and Pontypridd became known as 'the Petticoat Lane of the Valleys'.

Market Street, *c.* 1950. In spite of the savage economic decline experienced by Pontypridd in the 1920s and 1930s, the market has survived in very much its original format. The Market Co. has resisted the temptation for wholesale development, opting instead for gradual refurbishment of the original buildings, retaining both indoor and outdoor markets in their traditional style.

Above: J. Hepworth & Son clothiers on the corner of Market Street and Church Street.

Below: Market Street, *c.* 1970. Since 1985 Pontypridd Market has undergone considerable change. The Lesser Town Hall was refurbished and opened as a market hall in 1988, and the outdoor market was extended in 1988 onto a site adjoining Church Street and St Catherine's Street.

Pontypridd outdoor market, *c.* 1970. Pontypridd market attracted people of the town and surrounding valleys and visitors from all parts of the country. The Victorians, and later the Edwardians, flocked to Pontypridd in trains and horse-drawn brakes or buses, carriages, gigs, traps, hansom cabs and four-wheel cabs. They came on horseback and in donkey carts to buy produce and goods at bargain prices from the market stallholders and town shopkeepers. Cattle and sheep were sold in the present-day fruit and vegetable market near its Church Street end. Early drovers to the town knew Church Street and Market Street together as Cattle Lane.

Pontypridd outdoor market, *c.* 1970. There were no street stalls in the early Victorian years but, with the increasing popularity and importance of the market, a Saturday indoor general produce market was introduced in 1887 in addition to the traditional Wednesday market. There was an indoor market which sold mainly agricultural produce in Pontypridd as early as 1805. It was held for many years on the ground floor of a square-shaped building with an arched, stone-tiled roof standing in Market Square at the lower end of the now demolished Arcade and beside the stable yard wall of the one-time New Inn Hotel.

Above: A view of the Co-Op Arcade, *c.* 1970. The Co-operative Movement was attracted to the area in 1898 and the Co-op came to Market Square, eventually taking over the whole of the Arcade until 1984 when it was demolished. The Arcade itself was built in 1890 on the area where once stood several forges where blacksmiths and farriers worked the hammer on their anvils.

Above: Pontypridd, c. 1910. On the right is the entrance (through the railings) to Ynysyngharad Park and the old road to the Chain Works. The horse and cart is about to cross the bridge over the Merthyr-Cardiff canal. On the left (but not shown) is the Llanover Arms. All the buildings in the foreground (and the canal) have disappeared, and on the site now is the roundabout providing access to the A470 dual carriageway.

Right: Butcher Arthur Lougher and his stall in Pontypridd Market, *c.* 1900.

Opposite below: A Taff Vale Railway Co. delivery outside the Boot & Shoe Exchange in Market Square near the flight of steps leading to Taff Street, *c.* 1905.

The corner of Market Street and Taff Street, *c.* 1945.

Shoppers bustling through Market Street to Taff Street on a busy Saturday or Wednesday, *c.* 1940.

Above: Clothing store Gwilym Evans on Taff Street. It also had a second entrance on the floor above leading to Market Street. The site was once occupied by Thompson and Shackell's music saloon, built in 1890.

Right: Taff Street, *c.* 1905. From 1875 the town boasted five collieries, three breweries, woollen factories, brickworks, mills and a chemical works. Two companies that had been established and important to the town's development were the Pontypridd Gas & Light Co. and the Pontypridd Water Works Co.

PAIGE
PAIGE
SALE · SALE · SALE · SALE · SALE · SALE ·
EDWARDS
SPORTSMANS

Opposite above: The corner of Market Square and Taff Street showing the newly designed shopping area in what was once the New Inn Hotel. Originally a farmhouse dating from the 1730s with a thatched roof, it later became the premier hotel in the town, boasting a magnificent staircase by 1922, built for £750 with a view of the grand stained-glass window beyond. In May, 1857, the New Inn was taken over by John George Cousins and under his tenancy, the pub's Long Room, later called the Assembly Room was opened, where petty sessions of Llanwonno and Ystradyfodwg were held. The building was extended in 1893, but sadly demolished in 1981 making way for a series of shops.

Opposite below: The toy department of Leslie's Stores, Taff Street. The imposing much-loved five-storey store was the most famous of Pontypridd's 'multiple stores'.

Above: The fire at Leslie's Stores, Taff Street, 1951. Sadly it marked the end of one of Ponty's famous landmarks.

Right: Mill Street looking towards Taff Street, *c.* 1968.

Taff Street looking towards the County Cinema, *c.* 1965.

The corner of Taff Street and Mill Street, *c.* 1920. At one time grocer Griffith Evans was at No. 1 Taff Street at the corner of Mill Street and John Crockett's shops were at Nos 2 and 3. Crockett was a prominent citizen and a partner of the Penygraig Coal Co. The shops were jewellers, pawnbrokers and ironmongers. They were also highly reputable cabinet makers, upholsters and polishers who supplied cradles for the new born and shrouds and coffins for those faithful departed.

Above: Flannel Mill, Mill Street, This is a lithographic impression of the three mills which flourished during the nineteenth century. The flannel mill became the property of the James family, composers of the Welsh National Anthem, *Hen Wlad Fy Nhadau*.

Below: Direct Trading Co., Taff Street, *c.* 1910. To the left of the store is the entrance to Ynysangharad War Memorial Park. The original footbridge was built in the summer of 1897, and it was proposed to build it opposite the Arcade from Market Square, but instead the lane next to the Butchers Arms Hotel was chosen. In 1923 a concrete bridge was built, only to be severely damaged by flooding and rebuilt in October 1991.

Mill Street bustled with craftsmen from the early Victorian era. In medieval times it was a rough track to Llanwonno, passing Gelly Fynaches Farm and the convent above Graigwen. With the coming of the railways in 1840, the Taff Vale Railway bridged the river Rhondda upstream and an arch on the bank near the Welsh Harp spanned the road, overlooking a water mill in the field below. The street derived its name from various mills in the vicinity. This was the main road to the Rhondda before major changes took place to the traffic system in Pontypridd in 1967.

NEW INN HOTEL
PONTYPRIDD.

This old-established First-Class Hotel is replete wit every comfort for Families and Commercial Gentlemen

Situated in the centre of very Picturesque Scenery, affording very pleasant drives and walks.

ONLY A FEW MINUTES' WALK FROM THE

Far-famed One-Arch Bridge over the Taff, The Berw Waterfalls, The Noted Rocking Ston and Druidical Remains, &c.

Also, within easy distance of all the Great Collieries in the Rhonc Valleys.

BILLIARDS (TWO TABLES).

W. MORRIS, Proprietor

An advertisement for the New Inn Hotel, Taff Street, *c.* 1900. The glorious list of Pontypridd attractions includes Berw Waterfalls, William Edwards's bridge, the Rocking Stone and 'druidical remains'.

Above: Taff Street, *c.* 1900. To the left is the New Inn Hotel and opposite is the Park Hotel. Also on the right was the Butcher's Arms Hotel which became part of the Park Hotel.

Below: Taff Street showing the Park Hotel on the right, *c.* 1910. During the Victorian era the building on the immediate left (now occupied as a bank) stood the Victorian Cloth Hall, a large drapery, general outfitting and hat and cap warehouse. All branches of tailoring were carried out on the premises owned before 1870 by Maria Jones and afterwards by John Daniel Jones.

High Street, *c.* 1970. Notice the newly developed shops along what was once the River Rhondda Bridge. At one time High Street leading to the Tumble was linked to Taff Street by the bridge which had iron parapets allowing views of the river.

Humphreys Garages Pontypridd Ltd, 1964. Situated at the top end of Mill Street, it had its own impressive car showroom and was also a popular coach hire business.

Marks & Spencer, Taff Street. The store opened on 22 February 1939 and was built over the river, opening onto the River Rhondda Bridge.

The Greyhound Inn on the Tumble, *c.* 1890. Public houses have played a major role in the history of the town and there's always been a huge variety to choose from. Some of the familiar inns included the Volunteers, Bluebell, White Hart, Cross Keys, Clarence, Greyhound, Criterion, Bunch of Grapes, Victoria, Castle, Taff Vale, Horse and Groom, Wheatsheaf, Prince of Wales, New Inn, Butchers Arms, Maltsters, Ivy Bush, Bridge Inn, Tredegar Arms and the Somerset.

A bus operating on High Street. The Pontypridd Urban District Council operated both single and double-decker trolley buses and had advantages over the tram service in that it was not confined to a track; it loaded and unloaded passengers at the kerb side and not in the roadway, and was quieter and smoother in operation. Trolley buses were also cheaper to run than petrol buses and gave off no fumes. The trolley bus could manoeuvre easily and give way to traffic that the tram so often held up in Taff Street.

The White Hart, 1970. This public house was used as a county court in 1851 and kept by Thomas Jones. In later years George Parfitt was the long-serving landlord and took care of the large billiard room and bar. In later years Tom Jones made his last performance in Pontypridd there (as Tommy Scott and the Senators) before leaving for London to record his first hit, *It's Not Unusual* in 1964.

The Tumble/Station Square, *c.* 1979. The Clarence Hotel was built in the 1890s and became the first permanent theatre in the South Wales coalfield, with the ability to seat an audience of a thousand. Built by John Trenchard and later run by Byron Charles, it was fitted with gas lighting, therefore ensuring a total ban on smoking inside. It was renamed the New Theatre and extended in 1901. Further extensions took place in 1938 when it became the County Cinema. It is now known as Angharad's and houses a popular bingo hall.

The Half Moon and the former Amelias, *c.* 1978. During the latter part of the nineteenth century the building to the left of the pub was a coffee shops run by James Coombes, a well-known Market Street restauranteur. The Half Moon was held under a lease granted in 1847 and was sold in 1899 to the Rhondda Brewery Co. for £2,500. Samuel Stanbury became the landlord.

Half Moon Bar, 1958. The bar, close to the entrance to Pontypridd Railway Station claimed to be the busiest pub in Wales. Pictured are Mrs Coles (left) and hostess Mrs Barnett. The Half Moon was closed in 1989 and later demolished to accommodate the new traffic system through Pontypridd.

Pontypridd Post Office on the Tumble. In 1840 the first post office opened in Pontypridd kept by a grocer named Thomas on Pentrebach Road. Before the Taff Vale Railway arrived mail for the town came by riders on horseback and to the Duke of Bridgewater Arms by coach until it stopped running between Merthyr and Cardiff in 1843. Mail for the Rhondda was at first collected by Shon Waun Adda who carried letters in a donkey cart. Charles Bassett was postmaster from 1843-1875 when he was succeeded by George Hughes and in 1880 by Alfred James MacMurray. The post office was situation in Market Street until it moved to a new main office at The Tumble. In 1900 the Pontypridd Post Office Choir was well known in the area. The post office pictured closed and transferred business to Mill Street and the building was transformed into a public house.

Postmaster Charles Bassett, *c.* 1860. Mr Bassett was a prominent figure in the commercial and public life of Pontypridd during the mid-nineteenth century. He was a founder member of the Pontypridd Market Company, established in 1877. He came to Pontypridd about 1840 and rapidly established a large business as a chemist, one the first of its kind in the town. He later became manager of the Provincial Banking Corporation and gave evidence in 1844 to the Royal Commission investigating the causes of the Rebecca Riots. He also assisted in founding the first permanent Wesleyan place of worship in Pontypridd at Chapel Street. In 1843 he was appointed postmaster at a time when the weekly volume of letters was no more than 400. It was due to this role as postmaster that Bassett became responsible for the adoption in 1856 of Pontypridd as the name for the growing town. It was said he had grown tired of having to deal with mail intended for the many other 'Newbridges' in Britain and Ireland. One of the main roads in neighbouring Llantrisant is still called Newbridge Road. He died in 1887 at his home at Brynffynnon on Merthyr Road.

Dewi Sant Hospital, Albert Road, Graig, *c.* 1975. Work commenced on the hospital in 1965 and cost over one million pounds to build. It was officially opened by Mrs K. Robinson, wife of the Rt Hon. Kenneth Robinson Minister of Health, on Tuesday 24 September 1968. The hospital was built on the site of the Graig Union Workhouse, a planning blunder in many ways since many elderly patients refused to be treated at Dewi Sant because they still regarded it as a workhouse and knew of the stigma this represented.

Horse & Groom, High Street, Graig. One of many public houses in Pontypridd that no longer exists, the Horse and Groom was demolished following development of the road leading from Pontypridd train station.

Shoni's Pond at the foot of the Graig. This area has always been a firm favourite with Pontypridd folk, who either enjoyed swimming in the pond during the hot summer months or enjoying the many walks in the woodlands and surrounding fields.

Sardis Road Bus Terminus with the White Palace Cinema on the left. The terraced houses along Sardis Road were demolished in the mid-1960s to accommodate the new road improvements and for the building of the river Rhondda road bridge. Further along, the Ex-Servicemen's Club (Duffy's) was rebuilt in Maesycoed. The street was originally called Jones Terrace, later Taylor's Terrace, and housed the bus terminus for Cardiff, Porthcawl and all other southern routes.

The Wheatsheaf Inn. The pub was situated in Zoar Street but later demolished. This is certainly a nostalgic reminder of what once existed in the area. The multitude of pubs, including the Greenmeadow, Taff Vale, Horse and Groom, Union Houses and Jubilee Hall, have all gone.

Pontypridd Railway Station. Until the 1930s, Pontypridd had another station, just behind the modern day station, known as Pontypridd Graig Station. When Pontypridd station was built by the Taff Vale Railway in 1840 it was a third of a mile long making it the longest platform in the world. It was known as Newbridge Station from 1840 to 1891 before being renamed and was progressively remodelled during the nineteenth century. Its present appearance derives largely from reconstruction carried out between 1907 and 1914. Modernisation was carried out by British Rail about 1974 and in 1991.

Frank Mason & Co. Ltd, Pontypridd Railway Station. With more than 250 trains a day passing through the town, newspaper and refreshment stalls like this one – who also employed 'cigarette boys' to sell goods to passengers on the train – were immensely popular.

Demolishing the old Welsh Harp pub and building the new one on Mill Street, *c.* 1904. The original Welsh Harp was a small building demolished when alterations were made to the seven-arch railway viaduct over the Rhondda for the proposed electrification of the Pontypridd to Porth tramline. The new Welsh Harp pub eventually became one of many buildings that housed the *Pontypridd Observer* news offices and was later renamed the Millfield Hotel.

Pontypridd Railway line looking towards the Rhondda. Pontypridd was the 'gateway to the valleys' according to the rail company slogan. When Brunel carried out a feasibility study for the proposed railway in 1836, he had assumed that its main function would be to carry iron from Merthyr. No one had anticipated the rapid growth of the Rhondda coal trade which would follow the opening of a level at Gyfeillion, a mile or so up the valley from Newbridge, by Dr Richard Griffiths in 1790 and of another by Walter Coffin (1784-1867) at Dinas in 1807. But as the extraction of coal got under way in the years following, the town found that it was ideally placed for transporting it down to the coast, especially as the railway station, unlike the road and canal, was conveniently situated on the Rhondda side of the valley.

Sardis Road Police Station. In December 1839 an agreement had not yet been reached on the formation of the new county police, so instead a trial force of a superintendent and six constables was established in the region. The superintendent Thomas Morgan Lewis was appointed in January 1840. He had been a coldstream guardsman for a short time before joining the Metropolitan Police and was a flamboyant character, as he adorned himself with a forage cap of blue with 'scarlet welts on top and sides, gold band and crown, with gold tassel on top,' with a swallow tailed coats with scarlet cuffs, with collars embroidered in scarlet with 'Crown and number', costing £15. Superintendent Lewis chose to reside at Llantrisant before moving to Newbridge in August 1841 where the first constable was PC Philip Banner. At the time the town consisted of little more than one long street extending from the old bridge to the Tumble, with a few houses at Mill Street and along the tram road which ran through the present Sardis Road across the top of the Tumble towards Treforest. On the steep rise from the Tumble to Pencoedcae and on the other side of the new railway was a cluster of cottages, public houses and common lodging houses, which was to remain the toughest quarter of the town for many years. PC Banner and his colleagues had quite a problem on their hands for the rapidly changing character of the Taff Vale had introduced lawlessness and violence. The canal had created a 'floating' population of bargees and ostlers ready and willing to supplement their meagre earnings with robberies and larcency. The sinkers of new pits at Gyfeillion (Hopkinstown) and Dinas as well as the hordes of hard drinking 'navvies' engaged on railway construction work were always ready to resort to violence. PC 26 James Thomas was the first police officer to take up residence as sergeant in the newly provided police station in Sardis Road (then called the Tramroad) early in 1845, becoming superintendent of No. 2 (Newbridge) District of the force in 1847. The station at Sardis had accomodation for one resident Constable, an office for the district superintendent and two cells.

Pontypridd Police Station which was built in 1868 to replace the Sardis Road station. It was demolished in 1991 and cleared for the building of the St Catherine's Corner car park in 2007. Before the first station at Sardis Road was provided the solitary Pontypridd policeman used his house or lodging as the police station and secured a prisoner overnight by handcuffing him to the solid iron grate in the kitchen. If there were more than one prisoner he had to stay up with them overnight.

Above: Pontypridd police constables, *c.* 1901.
One of the problems faced by police constables at Pontypridd in the 1840s was stemming the uncontrolled influx into the country of hordes of Irishmen and Scotsmen, who together with their families, came seeking the better prospects of living afforded by the rapid growth of industry in Wales. It was the duty of the parish constables to bring the 'Irish or Scotch Poor' before the magistrates who were directed to send them back to the countries from which they came.

Right: The town crier, 1879. With cries of 'Oyez! Oyez!' he was a familiar site in the market town, relaying recent news from the vicinity to the passing crowds. In the 1880 *Slaters Commercial Directory* the town crier is named as Frederick J. Thomspon, and referred to as 'billposter and town crier'. By 1897 James Thyer boomed the same words while ringing his bell at the junction of Taff Street and Mill Street. It is uncertain which of these is pictured, but is most likely to be 'Thyer the Cryer' himself!

Samuel Palmer (left) and his brother Richard, who started a bus service between Pontypridd and Tynant in June 1921 with this fourteen-seater Ford nicknamed 'The Favourite'.

View towards Pontypridd Uniting Reformed church from Gelliwastad Grove.

Gelli Wastad House 1895. The farm was once owned by Dr Griffith's family who built the Machine Bridge and Doctor's Canal in Treforest. It also formed part of the estate inherited by Miss Clara Thomas, the well-known heiress of Llwynmadoc. She later bequeathed the house to the people of Pontypridd, which resulted in the opening of the Gelliwastad Institute in 1899.

Morgan Street pictured in 1967. This was another area of Pontypridd long-since forgotten and demolished under the banner of 'progress'.

Left: Dr Leckies house on Morgan Street. In earlier times Morgan Street was known as Ynysgyfeiliau ('island of smithies') because of the many forges there. Except for a few houses at its northern end, the street and its small courts like Matthews Court and Cooks Place, where a nailmaker's forge once stood, have been demolished to make way for the bus station and police headquarters.

Below: Ynysangharad House. Situated in Pontypridd's War Memorial Park, it was demolished in 1971. Originally the property of the Crawshay dynasty, it later passed by marriage to Sir Benjamin Hall, best remembered for having been commissioner for works in 1855, when the clock at the Houses of Parliament was built – the bell being named Big Ben. Hall was a tall, domineering character and probably the source of the naming of the bell. Ynysangharad House was later leased to Gordon William Lenox and Lewis Gordon Lenox JP, partners of the Brown Lenox chainworks and also by the firm's manager George James Penn. It was later the home of the Scudamore family and was extended in the 1920s to include Kenver House, with its main building becoming a clinic. The entrance was destroyed by fire during the 1950s.

Above: Llanover Arms and the West Street junction. It was a busy area for trams travelling out of Pontypridd. The Llanover was one of the oldest free houses in the town. The adjacent Crown Inn and later the Hinkley's Arcade, Mr Jeffrey's fruit shop, post office, fish shop and the Queen's Hotel have all been demolished.

Below: Lock No. 30 of the Glamorganshire Canal at Trallwn 1909. It was specially decorated for the arrival of Princess Louise on 23 August. This is also the site of Hinkley's Arcade which sold furniture and was sandwiched between the Llanover Arms and the Queens Hotel. Also in this area was the Crown Inn, which was run in 1900 by Elizabeth Evans who was fined 10s that same year for allowing illegal drinking on a Sunday.

Queen's Hotel, 1970. The demolition of this imposing building robbed Pontypridd of one of its most famous landmarks. The Queen's Hotel was demolished in 1971 to make way for the A470 dual carriageway which sliced through this section of Pontypridd, also taking a large section of Ynysangharad War Memorial Park and the defunct Glamorganshire Canal in the process.

The Duke of Bridgewater's Arms, Pentrebach Road. Better known as 'the Duke', it was a popular venue when mail coaches ran between Merthyr and Cardiff in the early nineteenth century.

two

An Industrial Capital

A bus travelling along the Glamorganshire canal at Trallwn, 1945. By the end of the eighteenth century the conditions for the preliminary phase of industrialisation in Newbridge were under way. The first significant event was the opening of the Glamorganshire Canal, from Merthyr to Cardiff, in 1794 – beforehand coal had to be carried to Cardiff by mule or in waggons over rough tracks. A barge could carry 24 tons and was worked by a horse, one man and a boy. The same amount would take twelve wagons, forty-eight horses, twelve men and twelve boys.

Glamorganshire Canal. For almost four years the navvies cut an astonishing 25-mile channel from Merthyr to Cardiff. The first major canal in Wales opened from Merthyr to Pontypridd in May 1792 and reached Cardiff in February 1794. Eventually it was completed in 1798 as it reached Cardiff docks. The entire project cost £103,600 and the Crawshay ironmasters were the main shareholders. A total of fifty locks were constructed in 25 miles of canal, which descended 160 feet in a mile from Quakers Yard and Abercynon.

Samuel Brown (1776–1852) founder of the Brown & Lenox Chainworks. Formerly of the Royal Navy, Samuel Brown patented a stud-link wrought-iron chain, suitable as ships' anchor cables and began manufacturing in 1803. To demonstrate the superiority of iron chains, Brown installed iron rigging and marine cables on a vessel called the *Penelope* and sailed to the West Indies. The admiralty were so impressed on his return in 1808 that they immediately ordered four vessels of war to be fitted with chain cables. It was to mark the beginnings of an unbroken series of annual contracts that lasted for over a century. In 1808 he formed a partnership with his cousin Samuel Lenox and they traded as Samuel Brown & Co. until 1823. The firms' anchor cables were adopted by the Royal Navy in 1810 and in 1812 the partners selected a site for their London works at Millwall followed in 1818 with an additional site at Pontypridd because of its proximity to the iron and coal industry.

Brown, Lenox & Co. Ltd advertisement. The chain works grew rapidly in size and reputation, and from the mid-nineteenth century were sole contractors to the Royal Navy for the supply of anchor chains. They also manufactured cables suitable for the construction of suspension bridges. The prestige of the contract brought orders from merchant shipping companies, passenger liners and leading engineers such as Thomas Telford and Kingdom Isambard Brunel. The factory closed in 2000.

Workers at Brown Lenox, *c* 1949. Isambard Kingdom Brunel (1806-59), who designed the Clifton Suspension Bridge and the three largest ships in the world, came to Pontypridd to buy the company's specially manufactured chains.

Workers at the Brown, Lenox & Co. chainworks. The firm made chains and anchors for many liners, including the *Lusitania*, the *Mauretania*, the *Queen Elizabeth* and the *Queen Mary*, and for the warships *Rodney* and *Nelson*. When German warships were scuttled at Scapa Flow in 1918, they were found to be equipped with chains and anchors made at Brown Lenox.

Workers at Brown Lenox with a long link wrought-iron chain with swivel.

Horses shunting coal wagons at Ty Mawr Colliery, 1905. Neighbouring Hopkinstown boasted the successful Great Western Colliery, sunk by railway engineer John Calvert in the 1860s. A period of expansion followed and by the late 1870s three more shafts had been sunk. During the 1880s, the Great Western Colliery became the largest pit in the Rhondda for manpower and output. However ten years later both shafts as well as the Old Ty Mawr Shaft were abandoned. A new Ty Mawr shaft (known as No. 1) was sunk and the Hetty Shaft retained to provide pumping and ventilation. The Powell Duffryn Steam Coal Co. Ltd later purchased Ty Mawr and owned it until nationalisation. In 1958 the National Coal Board invested £1.2 million in a surface and underground reorganisation to merge Ty Mawr with the Lewis Merthyr Colliery. All coal winding at Lewis Merthyr ceased as Ty Mawr was used for bringing the coal to the surface, with materials going down Lewis Merthyr. Production ceased in 1983.

A Maritime Colliery horse goes into retirement. Except for an annual two weeks per year ('Miner's Fortnight'), pit ponies rarely saw the light of day. The Maritime was opened by John Edmunds in 1841 after he sank a shaft 800 yards deep to the north of Gelliwion Colliery (sunk 1838) and at a depth of 60 yards he found and worked No. 3 Rhondda Seam.

Above: Miners from the Maritime Colliery. From 1875 to 1930 Maritime was part of the Great Western Colliery and became known as the Pontypridd Colliery. A new shaft was sunk in 1906 and by 1920 it employed 1,040 men, dwindling to 412 by 1959. It eventually closed in June 1961.

Below: A political meeting held at Y Maen Chwyf (or Rocking Stone), Pontypridd Common. Miners' agents and prospective Labour socialist candidate for East Glamorgan C.B. Stanton is seen here opening his election campaign on 9 June 1910. He came third and last in the election of December 1910 polling 4,675 votes. The seat was won by the Liberal candidate Clement Edwards.

Miners Protest, Pontypridd, 1910. The hunger marches, caused by strikes throughout the valleys and eventual Tonypandy riots, travelled to Pontypridd on 19 December 1910. After a trial lasting six days, a number of miners were tried and convicted of intimidation and assault on a miner they considered a blackleg. Two were sent to prison. The strike, called by the South Wales Miners Federation over a pay dispute, involved 12,000 men employed by the Cambrian group. It continued until September 1911 when the miners relented and went back to work, accepting the terms originally offered.

A steam train travelling to Pontypridd. In 1835 Anthony Hill, owner of the Plymouth Iron Works, asked his friend Isambard Kingdom Brunel, to estimate the cost of building a railway from Merthyr to Cardiff. Brunel's estimate was £190,649. Local industrialists held a meeting, chaired by John Josiah Guest, at the Castle Inn in Merthyr, to discuss the issue, and decided to request Parliamentary permission to form a company to build the railway. On 21 June 1836, Royal Assent was given to a The Taff Vale Railway Co.'s Act, allowing for the creation of the Taff Vale Railway Co. The founding capital of the company was fixed at £300,000, in £100 share units. The act capped the speed of the trains on the line to 12mph, with stiff penalties for any speeding. Construction of the railway was started in 1836, and the stretch from Cardiff to Abercynon was opened on 9 October 1840. The stretch from Abercynon to Merthyr was opened in April 1841. The line mostly followed the course of the valley, and therefore needed few bridges and no tunnels. Brunel designed an impressive skew stone arch viaduct at Pontypridd, which spanned 11ft over the River Rhondda.

A Pontypridd engine crew of fireman Garnet Lang, driver Owen Morgan and a third, unknown person in the early 1920s. In 1841, two branch lines were opened. The TVR entered the Rhondda with a four-mile 38-chain route from Pontypridd to Dinas, and the three-mile 29-chain Llancaiach branch was opened from Stormstown Junction (north of Pontypridd) to Llancaiach colliery. In 1849, the Rhondda branch was extended into Rhondda Fach, with a short line from Porth to Ynyshir. This was extended to Ferndale in 1856, and finally to Maerdy. The Rhondda Fawr line was extended from Dinas to Treherbert, also in 1856. The TVR proved its worth immediately. At its peak, two trains a minute passed through Pontypridd. By 1850, the TVR was carrying 600,000 tons of coal per annum, there were two passenger trains each way daily, including Sundays. This was extended to three weekday services in 1844. Single fares from Cardiff to Merthyr were 5s for first class, 4s for second class, and 3s for third, and were each reduced by 1s in 1845.

Female railway staff during the Second World War. With so many men enlisting in the armed forces, women employees were drafted in to Pontypridd Railway Station during the war years.

Train disaster near Pontypridd, 23 January 1911. Early that morning, at the height of the miner's strike, news spread of a rail crash at Hopkinstown. Many were dead and dozens were injured. Among the dead were three well-known miners' leaders, including councillors from Ferndale, Pontygwaith and Treherbert, along with a Methodist minister from Caerphilly. Passenger trains from the Rhondda were timed to leave the station at 9.40 a.m. for Pontypridd and Cardiff. While travelling at about 30mph towards the coke ovens, it crashed into a fully laden train from the Lewis Merthyr Colliery, which was stationary on the same track. Passengers were trapped, bodies hung through smashed windows and corpses were taken into the engine shed, where eleven of the dead were laid.

Taff Vale Railway Line and Pontypridd Tram Road Station, June 1922. Since the 1921 census the population of Pontypridd has been in continual decline. The town like many others in south Wales between the wars suffered from its dependence on coal. The decision of British and other navies to change from coal to oil proved disastrous for Welsh steam coal exports. With the coalfield in crisis, the number of collieries diminished and those that remained became increasingly cost-conscious. Pontypridd saw its prosperity dwindle and its population decline as many of its citizens were forced to seek a livelihood elsewhere. A significant development with the aim of bringing employment to the area was the establishment of the Treforest Trading Estate in 1936. By September 1939, 2,500 workers were employed at Treforest and between sixty to seventy firms were in production.

Hopkin Morgan, 1914. He was born in 1854 on the Graig where his father kept a grocery shop on High Street. Bread was baked at the shop by his mother but eventually a bakery was built further up the hill. Hopkin later opened a large steam-powered bakery in East Street, Trallwn and constructed a short length of canal to join the Glamorganshire Canal so that sacks of flour brought from Cardiff Docks could be delivered by barges direct to the bakery. He gave many private and public gifts and in the Christmas of 1897 sent a half-ton cake to the Cardiff Santa Claus Fund to be shared among 2,000 children in need. He became a Graig ward councillor and was chairman of the Pontypridd Urban District Council from 1914 to 1915 and chairman of the Welsh National Memorial Committee. Morgan was also the donor of the council chairman's chain of office and later became a justice of the peace.

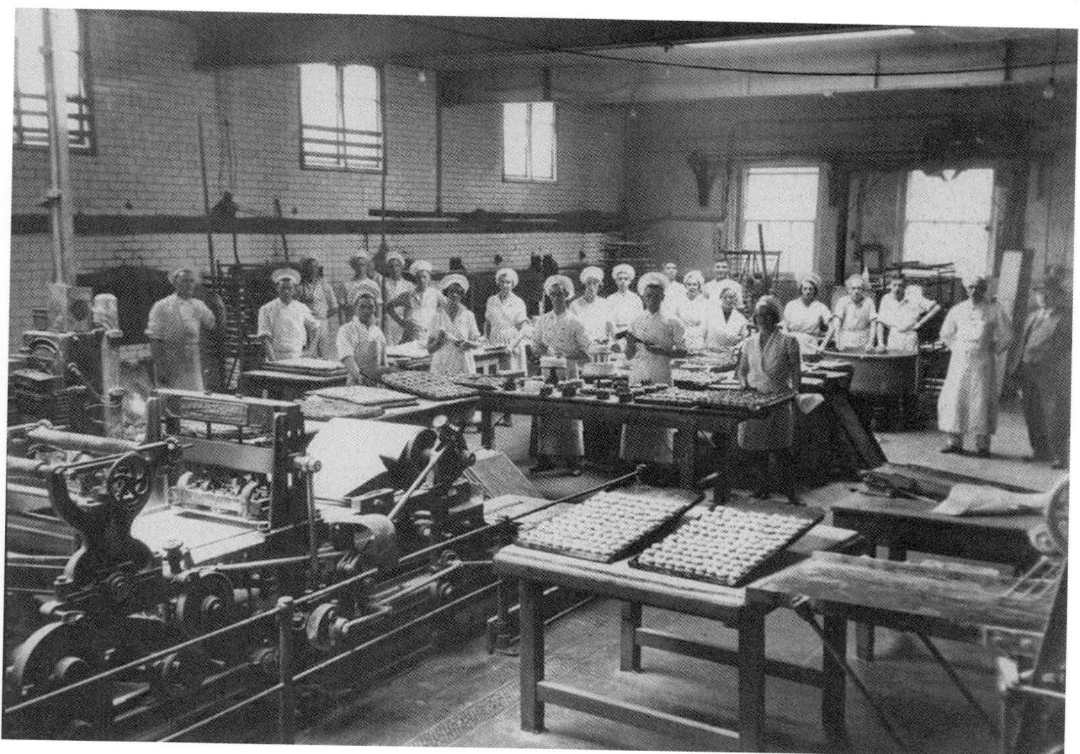

Interior of the Hopkin Morgan bakery at East Street, Trallwn. His main bakery shop was found at No. 74 Taff Street.

A Pontypridd Urban District Council trolleybus, *c.* 1948.

Historian Peter Gould wrote the following article on the history of public transport in Pontypridd:

The authority to construct a tramway in Pontypridd was given under the Pontypridd and Rhondda Valley Tramways Order of 1882, although by 1887 only a small section of the tramway, running from the edge of Pontypridd to the village of Porth, had been built by the tramway company. Solomon Andrews took over construction of the line from the Pontypridd and Rhondda Valley Tramways Company and it commenced operations later in the year. The tramway was single-track throughout and ran from The Square at Porth to the Taff Vale Railway's viaduct on the Rhondda line at Pontypridd, which prevented the Tramway Company's double-deck cars (and the line itself) from being extended further into the town. In 1890, however, the Company went into liquidation and was purchased by another of Andrews' concerns, the South Wales Property, Machinery and Carriage Company and operated until 1898 when it was sold to the British Electric Traction Company. The agreement of the local authorities to electrify and extend the line was not forthcoming and, in February 1902, after an attack of glanders killed most of the tramway horses, the services were terminated. Pontypridd UDC had already made plans to purchase and electrify the line, and work on the reconstruction had begun in July 1903 with an opening date set for March 1905. The Pontypridd and Rhondda Valley Tramways Co. was eventually purchased on 31 October 1904. The tramway officially opened on the 5th March 1905 and ran from the town centre to Treforest railway station, with a branch line connecting to Cilfynydd, which was worked as a single route via Pontypridd. In 1908 the tramway was connected to the Rhondda system at the Trehafod boundary, where passengers were required to change cars until July 1919 when through running commenced, although this was abandoned in December 1927 after endless disagreements between the two towns. By this time, however, the Pontypridd system was experiencing difficulties; the Cilfynydd line was in need of expensive refurbishment, which the small town could ill afford and plans were made to replace the trams. In 1929 Pontypridd UDC obtained powers to operate motorbuses and trolleybuses, and, on eighteenth September 1930, the Treforest to Cilfynydd section was converted to trolleybus operation. Seven single-deck 32-seat English Electric trolleybuses (Nos. 1-7) formed the initial fleet. The following year, on 30th August 1931, the remaining line to Trehafod was closed and motorbuses took over, the through service to Porth being operated jointly with Rhondda. The first motorbus service had commenced in June the previous year when a service between Pontypridd and Rhydfelin had been inaugurated using four Bristol B-type single-deckers. The Bristol chassis subsequently became a regular choice for Pontypridd UDC. The new trolleybus service proved extremely popular, so much so that at busy periods it was necessary to supplement the trolleybuses with tramcars, and so the exact date of the last tram is uncertain. As a result additional trolleybuses were soon purchased and in early 1931 a pair of demonstrators arrived. The first was a Guy BTX with Guy H59R bodywork, followed shortly afterwards by a Bristol E with Beadle H60R bodywork, one of only two ever built. Both demonstrators were purchased in 1932.

The trolleybus service was now established and continued unchanged until the advent of the Second World War, when wartime demands saw several trolleybuses arrive on loan. Further motorbus services were established throughout the 1930's, principally to Caerphilly (jointly with Caerphilly UDC), to Ynysybwl (jointly with Rhondda and Red & White) and to the Treforest Trading Estate, which was established to entice alternative industries to the area in view of the high unemployment in the coal mining industry. In 1945 Pontypridd ordered eight Karrier trolleybuses to replace the ageing fleet, and these were delivered over a period commencing with Nos. 10-11 (FNY983-984) in March 1945 and ending with the arrival of Nos. 8-9 (GNY301-302) towards the end of 1946. The business of Jones Brothers of Treharris, who were operating stage services from Pontypridd to Blackwood and to Bedlinog, along with two vehicles and works services to Pontllanfraith was acquired in 1945, jointly with three neighbouring authorities. In 1950 the Transport Manager drew the Council's attention to the economics of maintaining such a small fleet of trolleybuses, and, with little prospect of expansion it was suggested that motorbuses would be more viable. As it happened no action was taken at this juncture, but the question was raised again in 1954, when the operating costs of the trolleybuses was shown to be around 3d a mile more than motorbuses. Again the matter was deferred since the extra running costs were considered to be too marginal to warrant expenditure on additional motorbuses. In 1955, however, with the trolleybuses regularly being replaced by motorbuses when out of service, the Council again debated the future of the trolleybuses and this time agreed that the system should be abandoned from the 31st October 1956. In the event, delays in the delivery of new motorbuses meant that the final abandonment did not take place until 31st January 1957; all the vehicles being sold for service elsewhere. The existing Rhydfelin service was linked to the Cilfynydd service, and the Treforest section became a single-deck route. New vehicles arriving in the fleet over the next few years included the AEC Reliance, which was to become the standard single-deck vehicle, whilst the AEC Regent V was purchased as the standard double-decker. With passenger numbers falling, a move to one-man operation was proposed that necessitated the linking of several services previously operated independently. Double-deckers were thus usually confined to school journeys, and to the principal routes to Glyncoch and Rhydfelin, although eventually these too were converted. Subsequently all new vehicles were capable of one-man operation and included a number of Leyland Nationals. In October 1969, rationalisation of the bus network took place, with Pontypridd taking over sole operation of the route to Glyncoch, whilst the Porth service was handed over to Rhondda Transport and the Ynysybwl service to Red & White. Pontypridd also relinquished their journeys on the former Jones Brothers routes, which were essentially loss making. Under local government re-organisation, which took place in 1974, Pontypridd UDC became Taff-Ely District Council. The Transport Department was little changed but assumed the name of the new District Council. In 1983 a number of second-hand Atlanteans enabled most of the AEC Regents, which were unsuitable for one-man operation to be withdrawn. On the 26th October 1986 the enactment of the 1985 Transport Act led to the Council setting up an 'arms-length' limited company known as Taff-Ely Transport Ltd., effectively ending municipal services after over 80 years, although the Council still retained the majority shareholding.

A Pontypridd Tram, *c.* 1910.

Above: Arrival of a First World War tank to Pontypridd, 1918. The tank was named 'Julian' and served in the war before coming to Pontypridd in May 1918 by rail. It was paraded through the town followed by a procession of several thousand. It came to a halt at the Fair Ground, opposed the YMCA and was welcomed by Cllr William Phillips of Pontypridd Urban District Council.

Below: Building Pantygraigwen Road, Pontypridd.

Ceremonial funeral procession going towards St Catherine's church on Gelliwastad Road. Notice the amount of police constables lining the main street.

St David's Presbyterian church on Gelliwastad Road was built in 1883 by Henry C. Harris of Cardiff. Before the sinking of the deep seam collieries, a substantial proportion of those attracted to Pontypridd to find work came from parts of rural Welsh counties. This initial influx resulted in the building of Nonconformist chapels where Welsh was the language of worship. Howell Harris had probably first kindled the Nonconformist flame in Pontypridd when he visited in 1739 but not until 1810 was Carmel Baptist chapel built, the first place of worship erected in the town. The first Calvinistic Methodist chapel was Penuel in Taff Street built in 1833. Sardis congregational chapel, was built in 1834. St Mary's church, Glyntaff was established in 1843 but not until 1868 with the building of St Catherine's church did Pontypridd have a church at the heart of the town.

Interior of Uniting Reformed church, Gelliwastad Road. The date stone is 1887 and it was built as an English congregational church in 1888 to the design of Potts, Sulman and Gemmings – the same firm that added the church hall in 1906.

Municipal Hall. Built in 1848 as a Wesleyan church and school and designed by local architect Arthur O. Evans, the site is now home to the Muni Arts Centre. An Urban District Council based on six wards was formed in 1895 replacing a local board that had governed the town between 1875 and 1895. The council had a number of statutory undertakings and provided its ratepayers with electricity, gas and transport services, in addition to public libraries, a park and recreation grounds and an open-air swimming bath.

Above: Sisterhood of the Wesleyan Methodist church of Gelliwastad Road, early 1930s.

Below: Demolition of Carmel chapel, Graigwen, 1969. There had been a proliferation of Nonconformist chapels, where Welsh was the main language of worship, since 1810, when Carmel Baptist church was built on Graigwen. It was the resting place of National Anthem composer Evan James.

Reburial of Evan James on Sunday, 1 July 1973 at the base of the memorial in Ynysangharad Park following the demolition of Carmel chapel, Graigwen. His wife, Elizabeth James was also exhumed from the destroyed Memorial Garden at Carmel before Plas Carmel flats were built, early the previous Sunday. Standing, left to right: Revd L. Haydn Lewis (Ton Pentre), Emlyn Lewis (officiating) of Hopkinstown and Mr W.T.H. Gilmore, founder of the Memorial Garden. Also pictured is Cllr Idris Griffiths, chairman of Pontypridd Council.

Pontypridd Cottage Hospital. The hospital was erected on the Common in 1910 and supported by voluntary subscription. The site was given by Miss Clara Thomas and the memorial stones were laid by the Viscount Tredegar on 5 May 1910. Miss Thomas opened it on 27 February 1911.

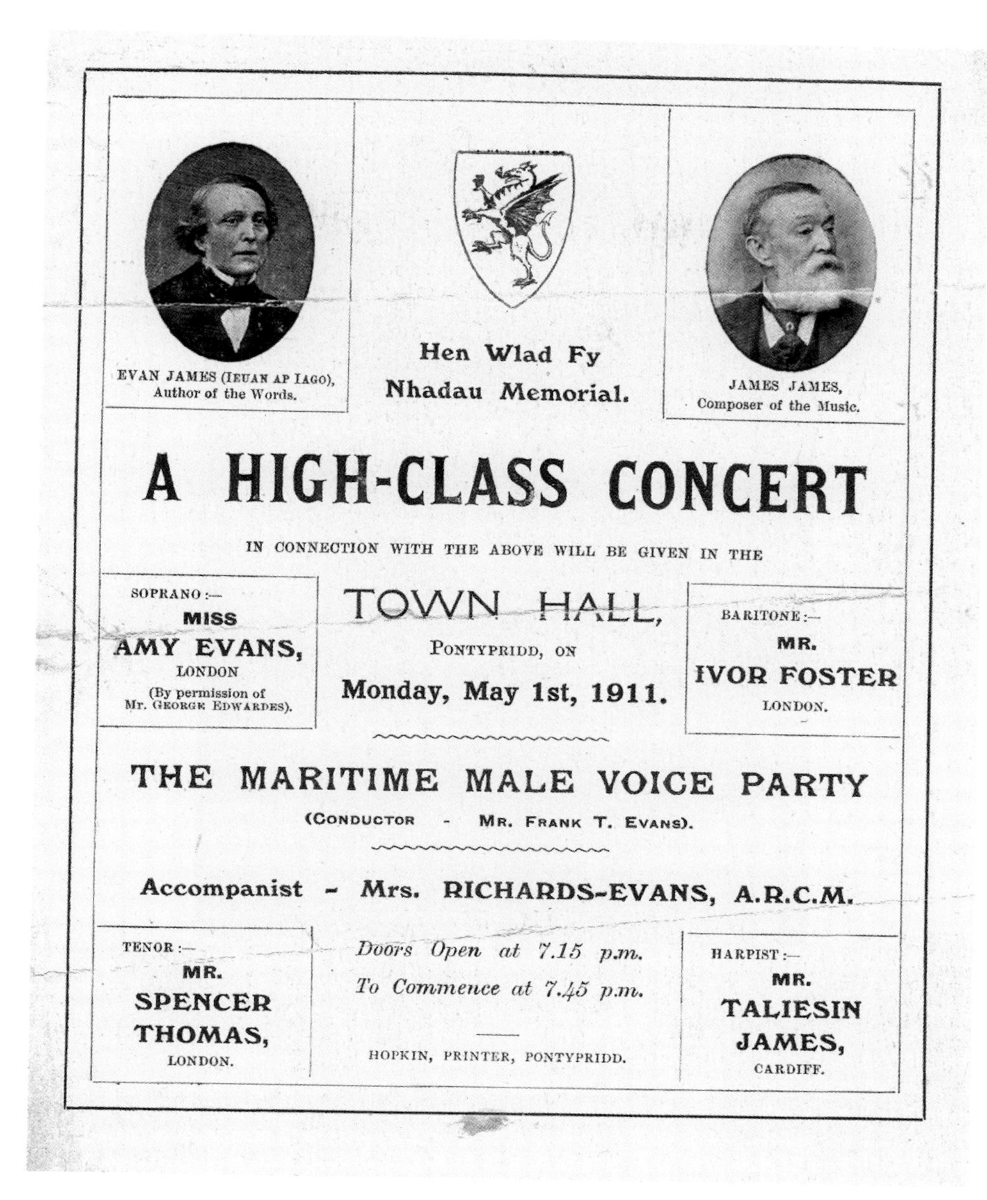
EVAN JAMES (IEUAN AP IAGO), Author of the Words.

Hen Wlad Fy Nhadau Memorial.

JAMES JAMES, Composer of the Music.

A HIGH-CLASS CONCERT

IN CONNECTION WITH THE ABOVE WILL BE GIVEN IN THE

SOPRANO :— MISS AMY EVANS, LONDON (By permission of MR. GEORGE EDWARDES).

TOWN HALL, PONTYPRIDD, ON Monday, May 1st, 1911.

BARITONE :— MR. IVOR FOSTER LONDON.

THE MARITIME MALE VOICE PARTY

(CONDUCTOR - MR. FRANK T. EVANS).

Accompanist - Mrs. RICHARDS-EVANS, A.R.C.M.

TENOR :— MR. SPENCER THOMAS, LONDON.

Doors Open at 7.15 p.m.
To Commence at 7.45 p.m.

HOPKIN, PRINTER, PONTYPRIDD.

HARPIST :— MR. TALIESIN JAMES, CARDIFF.

'A High-Class Concert' held at Pontypridd Town Hall to raise funds for the proposed memorial to Evan and James James, 1 May 1911. One of the musicians is none other than harpist Taliesin James, along with the Maritime Male Voice Party (conductor Frank Evans) and selected soloists. Inside the programme the first announcement reads: 'Please Note: All Ladies are respectfully requested to take off their hats' presumably to ensure better vision of the stage for those sitting behind!

Dr William Price (1800-1893) painted in 1821 by Alexander Steward. Chartist, surgeon, heretic, archdruid and pioneer in the legalisation of cremation in the British Isles. Dr William Price was undoubtedly one of the most flamboyant, romantic and eccentric characters in Welsh history. Born in Rudry in 1800, he became a rather brilliant scholar, studying at the London Hospital and becoming a surgeon by the age of just twenty-one. In 1827 he became the surgeon of the Brown Lenox chainworks. Claiming to be the archdruid of Wales he was often seen carrying out ancient druidic rights on the Rocking Stone (Y Maen Chwyf). A leader of the failed Chartist Rising of 1839, he fled to France disguised as a woman. In 1860 he built the Round Houses at Glyntaff as the entrance to his new home and museum to druidism, but the venture failed. Known for his flamboyant head dress and costume, he opened the first co-operative societies in the county and was also responsible for an embryonic national health service for the workers. In 1871 he moved to Llantrisant with his housekeeper who was sixty years his junior and the couple had three children. The first, named Iesu Grist (Jesus Christ) died after five months and he attempted to cremate the corpse, causing mayhem in the town. In March 1884 he conducted his own defence at the Cardiff Crown Court trial over the cremation, claiming it was not right to allow a carcass to rot in the ground and pollute the earth. He was acquitted by Justice Stephens, making way for the passing of the Cremation Act of 1902. After sipping a glass of champagne, he died at the age of ninety-three and was cremated in Llantrisant. A crowd of 20,000 turned out for the event and a carnival atmosphere prevailed throughout the town.

A gravestone remembers Philip Thomas, the first manager of the chainworks. The story behind the stone that overlooks his workplace on the Common has become part of the folklore history of Pontypridd. When he died in 1840, Glyntaff church had just been completed and he was the first to be interned there. The lack of a stone over his grave caused some annoyance to Francis Crawshay, well-known resident of Forest House and manager of Treforest Tinplate Works. He therefore took it upon himself to erect a grave stone at Glyntaff but Thomas's family took exception to the epitaph's ambiguity. Indeed, they were so incensed that they removed the stone and left it lying in a nearby field. Dr William Price came upon it and with the assistance of Crawshay, arranged for it to be placed in its present position near the druidic circle. The name Philip Thomas has been erased from the stone:

> Stranger Halt! I am placed here to commemorate the virtue and abilities of who after managing the chain work on my right hand side for the space of 21 years much to the benefit of all mankind died and was buried herein 1840 aged 69.

Snow scene at The Fountain, 1947. The well-documented blizzards of 1947 brought most of the country to a standstill. Pontypridd certainly suffered one of the worst snowstorms in living memory. For two days the snow continually fell and became piled into drifts by the high wind, bringing the rail and bus network to a halt.

Snow scene in Taff Street, 1947. Hundreds of colliers and factory workers were unable to reach their workplaces and Pontypridd Market closed its doors. Petrol buses replaced the trolley cars between Cilfynydd and Treforest under orders from the PUDC.

Snow scene in Taff Street, 1947. Although Taff Street is depicted as a no-go area, Cilfynydd, Maesycoed, Graig and Graigwen suffered the worst from the inclement weather where householders literally had to dig themselves out. No trains could run to Caerphilly owing to drifts in Nantgarw and Groeswen and church services, along with local dances were all cancelled.

Snow scene in Taff Street, 1947. Absenteeism in the local collieries were as high as seventy per cent. At the Albion Colliery 200 miners were absent out of 320, but it was decided to carry on. Cwm and Ty Mawr Collieries saw seventy per cent of its workforce absent while Lewis Merthyr was down by 60 per cent.

Snow scene on The Tumble, 1947. Treforest Trading Estate saw a huge reduction in its workforce during the blizzard. Only half of the 9,000 employees reached the factories on the first day of the snowfall. By the second day only ten per cent turned up. The local paper explained, 'The management of one factory sent a van and a car to take employees home to Gilfach Goch and both vehicles were snowed under. The drivers were given hospitality for the night in a miner's cottage.'

PONTYPRIDD
OBSERVER

SATURDAY JANUARY 26th. 1935.

PONTYPRIDD PROTESTS
DEMONSTRATIONS AGAINST UNEMPLOYMENT ACT

HOSPITAL BALL
LIST OF GUESTS

"THE MESSIAH" AT CILFYNYDD

DEATH OF MRS. C. BASSETT
HOPKINSTOWN'S GRAND OLD LADY

PENTYRCH HUNT FARMERS BALL

CILFYNYDD
WIFE'S ALLEGATIONS
Husband Accused of Persistent Crueltv

Left: *Observer* news bill, January 1935. During the 1870s Archibald Allan McLucas established *The Pontypridd District Herald* which was printed at its offices in Mill Street. Benjamin Davies bought it out to create *The Pontypridd Chronicle* which in turn was purchased by *The Glamorgan Free Press*. The first issue of *The Observer* was printed on 20 March 1897 and cost ½d. It later had an office and printing works at No. 77 Taff Street and was edited by Percy Phillips up until the Second World War when he was killed in a road accident.

Below: A rare photograph of a double-decker bus which came off the road at Zion Street and plunged into the Taff riverbank.

Cutting of the first sod of the site for the YMCA, 25 March 1909. The councillor who was invited to dig the first spade into the ground was none other than local baker Hopkin Morgan.

Crowning of the Cottage Hospital beauty queen by chairman of Pontypridd Urban District Council, William Jones, July 1935.

Above: Election Day at Pontypridd, *c.* 1905. Pictured is David Evans of Rhydyfelin along with James Roberts JP, the first chairman of the Pontypridd UDC. In the centre of the picture is journalist Owen Morgan, better known as Morien (1836-1921). Rhondda-born Morien settled in Glyntaf and was the local journalist for *The Western Mail*. He specialised in the reporting of mining disasters, and wrote from around 1870 until his death in 1921 about the local traditions of druidism. Something of a local character himself, Morien wrote a number of books which include *Pabell Dafydd* (1889), about the Druids, *Kimmerian Discoveries*, on the alleged Chaldean origins of the Welsh, *A Guide to the Gorsedd* and *A History of Pontypridd and the Rhondda Valleys* (1903). The latter, described by R.T. Jenkins as 'an odd jumble of Druidism, mythology, topography, local history and biography' is one of the most unreliable local history books of the time.

A fancy-dress carnival held at the Alexandra Hall skating rink, Pontypridd, 1909.

River Rhondda Bridge, High Street, showing the Temple of Fashion and the local fire brigade, *c.* 1900. During this period High Street was occupied by M. Davies Art Depot which sold fine silks and wools along with J.E. Brooks, hairdresser and tobacconist, where a haircut cost 3d and patrons could also take hot and cold baths.

Opposite below: Danters annual Easter Monday Fair opposite the YMCA, Taff Street, April 1938. It was held in the Fairfield, a field owned by brewer Capt. Williams.

Above: Preparations for an outing to the seaside in front of the Clarence Hotel, 1907.

Below: Gwilym Evans staff daytrip 1952.

Opposite above: The arrival of King George and Queen Mary to Pontypridd, June 1912. Trams were specially decorated in June 1911 for the coronation of the King and Queen, who stopped off briefly at Pontypridd station while on a visit to the Rhondda and Merthyr.

Below: Staff of the Pontypridd Workhouse on the Graig. Pontypridd Poor Law Union was formed in December 1862. Its work was overseen by a twenty-five-strong Board of Guardians. A new Pontypridd workhouse was erected in 1865 at the south side of Court House Street. It was designed by G.E. Robinson and construction cost £7,000. The original building was a T-shaped block. By 1900 the workhouse had greatly expanded with an infirmary and isolation hospital, together with further blocks on High Street. There were 320 inmates there by the turn of the twentieth century. The workhouse later became known as Central Homes and then under the NHS as Graig Hospital for the chronic sick. The original buildings were demolished in the mid-1960s and a new hospital called Dewi Sant was built on the site.

SUNDAY, 10th JUNE, 1956

TOWN HALL THEATRE, PONTYPRIDD

7.45 p.m.

CELEBRITY CONCERT

ARTISTES

VICTORIA ELLIOTT (Soprano) — ROWLAND JONES (Tenor)

Appear by permission of Sadlers Wells Trust Ltd

CONSTANCE SHACKLOCK (Contralto) — GERAINT EVANS (Bass Baritone)

Appear by permission of the Royal Opera House, Covent Garden, Ltd

Accompanist — EDWARD DOWNES

Supported by the

PONTYPRIDD Y.M.C.A. MALE VOICE CHOIR

(Conducted by GWILYM T. JONES)

The Programme will be introduced by

THE EARL OF HAREWOOD

Admission — 7/6; 5/- & 3/6 (All Seats Reservable)

Town Hall Celebrity Concert poster, June 1956. It was a year to remember in Pontypridd history marking the centenary of composing *Hen Wlad Fy Nhadau* and the bicentenary of William Edwards building his famous bridge. Schools, choirs, churches, chapels and rotary clubs all got together to make arrangements. *The Observer* sponsored an essay writing competition and Sir Geraint Evans held a concert in the town, attended by the Earl and Countess of Harewood. The BBC flocked to Ponty and the park was packed for seven full days. The main event began on 3 June with a service of celebration at the bandstand in the park. An evening hymn singing concert saw the Band of the 5th Battallion Welsh Regiment perform under Lt-Col. C.H. Allen. The Old Age Pensioners Association held a Festival of Song in a marquee and one of the most memorable moment was the 'Beating the Retreat' by the Welch Regiment band, followed by a full concert in the open air. There was a Welsh Day and a 'Noson Lawen'. On Thursday 7 June all eyes were turned on Taff Vale Park with the Pontypridd Secondary Schools' Sports Day, followed by a concert featuring the Boys' Grammar School pupils in Ynysangharad Park. The festivities with a major celebrity concert in the Town Hall Theatre featuring Geraint Evans, Constance Shacklock, Victoria Elliott and Rowland Jones.

Staff of Woolworth's, *c.* 1950. They were pictured at the rear of the store in Ynysangharad War Memorial Park.

John Hughes of the World of Groggs. John Hughes was born in February 1934 in Pontsionnorton. He attended Pontypridd Boys' County Grammar School before working at City Hall, Cardiff. In 1952 he began his National Service with the RAF until 1954. He was working in the College of Food Technology in 1965 when he retreated to his back-garden shed and created the very first of the Groggs. Becoming a hugely successful business based in a property on The Broadway, Treforest, his early works concentrated on the great Welsh rugby stars of the 1960s and 1970s. For over forty years he has created these unique caricature statuettes depicting everything from international singers and Hollywood actors to Welsh sheep and miners.

The Monument, Pontypridd Common. Erected in memory of the men of the 5th battalion of The Welch Regiment killed in the First World War, it was unveiled by Viscount Allenby on 6 August 1923. The Memorial names the twenty-eight officers, three warrant officers, fifty-one NCOs and 279 men of the battalion who died in the First World War.

Left: James Bye (1889–1962) of the Graig, Pontypridd. After leaving school he worked at the Deep Duffryn Colliery, Mountain Ash, before joining the Welsh Guards in 1915. He quickly progressed through the ranks and was promoted to lance-corporal in March 1916, corporal in September of that year and then sergeant in April 1917. He served in France and Flanders and was discharged in February 1919. Six months later he re-enlisted in the Notts and Derby Regiment, remaining with it until 1925, and finally re-enlisting again in the Sherwood Foresters in World War Two. He died in 1962, aged seventy-two and is buried at Warsop Cemetery, Nottingham. Sgt Bye received the Victoria Cross on 31 July 1917 following a battle at the Yser Canal, Belgium, where he displayed the utmost courage and devotion to duty during an attack on an enemy position. He was invested with his VC by King George V on 27 September 1917.

Below: Pontypridd Civic Sunday Service, 1938.

Wings for Victory week at the New Inn, on 14 May 1943. In order to encourage people to buy government sponsored savings bonds, savings stamps and certificates, Churchill's government used a series of advertising campaigns appealing to the public's patriotic instincts. It worked as by the end of 1945 savings bonds had raised £1,754 million for the war effort. Early in the war Lord Beaverbrook came up with the idea of 'presentation' aircraft where towns could organise events to help towards the cost of purchasing an aircraft bearing the name of the town or donor. Communities often competed against one another to see who could raise the most. These National Savings campaigns were usually for a week's duration and went under such titles as War Weapons Weeks, Warship Week, Salute the Soldier and Wings for Victory.

Armistice Parade along Taff Street. Unlike the people of many British towns and cities, Pontypridd residents did not have to emerge from their air-raid shelters to find that their houses were no longer standing, and to see demolished buildings in streets strewn with shattered glass, but the threat of imminent destruction was implicit in every warning air-raid siren. There were more than 300 night and day air-raid warnings in Pontypridd and its villages in the Battle of Britain of 1940 and many more air-raid warnings later on.

Above: Celebrating VE Day along Taff Street, 1945. Pontypridd was hit by a large number of incendiary bombs and thirteen high-explosive bombs, which dropped near the Lan Wood Reservoir and along Lan Park and Tyfica Road in August 1940. Several houses and villas suffered slight damage and some boundary walls collapsed. There were no deaths, but glass splinters caused a few minor injuries. Bombs fell in Hopkinstown and in Cilfynydd during other raids. People were killed in Porth and further up the Rhondda Valley in later bombing. Other than those differences in the intensity of air attacks, and constant doorstep scenes of other wartime drama in those valiant years, Pontypridd played its full part in the war.

Left: Wreaths being laid at the war memorial in Ynysangharad Park.

Above: Armistice Parade near Gwilym Evans store, Taff Street.

Right: Arthur Pearson CBE MP (1897-1980). Mr Pearson was elected the Labour Member of Parliament for Pontypridd at a 1938 by-election, and served until his retirement in 1970 before being succeeded by Brynmor John (who sadly died in 1988 at the age of just fifty-five). Mr Pearson was Controller of the Household from 1945-1946 and Treasurer of the Household from 1946-1951.

Above: Pontypridd Boys' Grammar School visit to Cheddar, 27 June 1937.

Below: Class 2B at Pontypridd Boys' Grammar, October 1950. Back row, left to right: P. Bewared, J. Rees, W. Hockey, T. Mullins, B. Lewis, A. Edwards, A. Canines, J. Caddy, L. Price, A. Ford. Middle row: C. Jones, J. Lewis, R. Pocket, G. Sage, B. O'Donnell, J. Elland, R. Pike, M. Gish, B. Arnold, C. West, N. Phillips. Front row: D. Bowen, K. Ball, R. Mahoney, J. Roberts, W. Davies, G. Powell, D. Short, P. Delbridge, P. Jarvis, P. Barwein, D. Beynsham. The form teacher was H. Meredith who taught music and English.

Pontypridd Boys' Grammar School, 1958. The history of the grammar school was dominated by Rhys Morgan, the first headmaster. In 1890 he opened the Heath School, (The Academy), on Gelliwastad Road. The name was probably connected to the philanthropic activities of the local landowner, George Thomas 'the Heath'. The first pupil registered at the Heath was Oswal Davies, who in 1901 bought up the business of Matthews the chemist in the Arcade. Following the passing of the Welsh Intermediate Education Act in 1889, plans went ahead to set up a new school.

Pontypridd Boys' Grammar School, 1958. By July 1891, progress was made with Lord Tredegar supplying 2 acres of land as a site and workmen of the Great Western Colliery donated £100 along with colliers from Ynysybwl. Ignatius Williams, stipendiary magistrate officially opened the Pontypridd County School, later the grammar school, on 25 September 1896. By June 1897 there were 105 boys and sixty-six girls on the school roll, with six travelling such a distance that they lived in 'approved lodgings'.

Pontypridd Girls' Grammar School. When Pontypridd Grammar School was twelve years old it was found necessary to plan the building of a new school for girls. In September 1908 a committee was formed and purchased land at Llanover Estate in Treforest.

Pontypridd Boys Grammar School, opened 1896. After a long and successful history the Grammar School became Coedylan Comprehensive School in 1973. Its motto was 'Effort in Pursuit of Success'.

Pontypridd Girls' Grammar School. The school was officially opened on 15 September 1913 by James Roberts JP, chairman of the Pontypridd Board of Governors.

Class 3B of Mill Street Secondary Modern School, November 1959.

Col. Lt Henry Llewellyn Grover, the first clerk to the Pontypridd Urban District Council (1845-1898). A well-known solicitor, his firm Grover & Grover was based in Mill Street with his brother Montague Grover. The colonel was born in Manchester and settled in Pontypridd with his wife Margaret and six children. They resided in Clydach Court, Llanwonno, a well-known Pontypridd landmark in its time which has since been demolished. The Grover name is also attributed to several areas between Pontypridd and Abercynon. He was later elected deputy coroner for the Borough of Cardiff in 1892. The PUDC based on six wards was formed in 1895 following the Local Government England and Wales Act of the same year. It took over the functions of Pontypridd Local Board of Health which had governed the town since 1875. The PUDC continued until March 1974 when it was merged with parts of Caerphilly Urban District and the rural districts of Llantrisant, Llantwit Fardre and part of Cowbridge to form Taff Ely Borough Council.

three

A Cultural Heartland

St Catherine's Church Choir, 1922

Pontypridd Royal Welsh Ladies' Choir, better known as Madam Muriel Jones' Choir. Founded in Treforest in 1927, they earned great reputation for performing for over almost thirty years – usually in traditional Welsh costume. During this time they sang for royalty on twenty occasions, including performances for Princess Helena Victoria in Pontypridd in July 1929, the Duke and Duchess of Kent in 1937 and the Duke (later George VI) and the Duchess of York at Windsor.

Madam Muriel Jones' Pontypridd Royal Welsh Ladies' Choir, pictured at St Donats as the welcoming party to its owner, William Randolph Hearst. The newspaper magnet was the basis of what many believe was the character in the film *Citizen Kane* played by actor Orson Welles.

Pontypridd and District Male Voice Choir, 15 April 1918. The conductor was David E. Phillips who joined them in 1896. In later years it was conducted by William John Evans (known as 'Stripes' because of his striped trousers) of Cilfynydd. Mr Evans had successfully conducted the local Handel Glee Party and Cilfynydd Male Voice Choir before coming to Pontypridd. His son was the world-famous opera star Sir Geraint Evans.

Above: Pantygraigwen Nightingales, 1926. This jazz band was formed during the Miner's Strike and helped raise funds through various competitions and performances. The conductor was Len Grubb and the band included many local children. At practice times the wives made costumes and covered cones with tissue paper to blow into. Whenever a competition was won, the men (and only the men!) were assured free beer at the Ty Mawr pub.

~ THE GREAT WESTERN COLLIERY SILVER PRIZE BAND. 1922.~

Above: Pontypridd YMCA Symphony Orchestra, 1924. The conductor was Brinley M. Lewis.

Below: Pontypridd Mixed Choir, 1910. Also known as the Treforest United Choir, it was conducted by Alun Dummer.

Opposite below: Great Western Colliery Silver Prize Band 1922. John Calvert, a railway engineer from Yorkshire, was one of the pioneers of the coal industry in the Rhondda. He was contracted to lay the Taff Vale Railway for Brunel but quickly noticed the vast profits of the emerging coal industry. He sank his first pit, Newbridge Colliery, in 1844 and became the first engineer to use steam power to raise coal. Four years later he sank Gyfeillion Colliery. Taking three years to reach the coal seam, it was the first pit to be sunk deeper than 100 yards. After leasing the pit for three months the Great Western Railway Co. purchased the colliery in 1854. Following ten very profitable years the company sold it back to Calvert. In 1866 he once more decided to sell the colliery. It was purchased by the Great Western Colliery Co. Ltd and became known as the Great Western Colliery.

Pontypridd Choral Society, *c.* 1953. Calvary Baptist church was founded in 1849 and a church choir was formed in the early years. By the 1930s it was known as the Calvary Augmented Church Choir, conducted by Gwyneth Lewis, the daughter of the minister for almost fifty years there, Revd Evan Lewis. She retired in 1967 and the choir's accompanist, Trevor Dummer became conductor, soon followed in the role by Brian Phills, the head of music at Pontypridd Girls' Grammar School who remained in the post for sixteen years. He was succeeded by Gill Shucker, Wynford Jones and more latterly Jeff Ryan, by which time it had changed its name to Pontypridd Choral Society.

The Shelley Singers. Eiddwen Griffiths-Davies was musical director of the Shelley Singers, named after the hall in Pontypridd where they practised. They gave their first performance in 1958 with Dorothy Ingram Davies as accompanist who remained in the post for many years. Four months after being formed they competed in the Llangollen International Eisteddfod and came fifth out of thirty-five groups. They were to enjoy considerable radio and television success becoming nationally admired through the TV programme *Aelwyd y Gan* and were the resident choir on BBC's *Croeso*.

Pontypridd Amateur Operatic Society. Drama societies thrived in the market town and even today the Pontypridd Theatre Co., which was formed in 1925, continues to play an active role in the community.

The 2nd Pontypridd Company, the Boys Brigade, 1964. The picture includes Revd Harold Bartlett and brigade captain Alan Williams who collapsed and died in the brigade room in 1970 when he was just thirty-six. He was succeeded by Paul Weston, who continued until the brigade, based at Calvary chapel disbanded in the early 1990s.

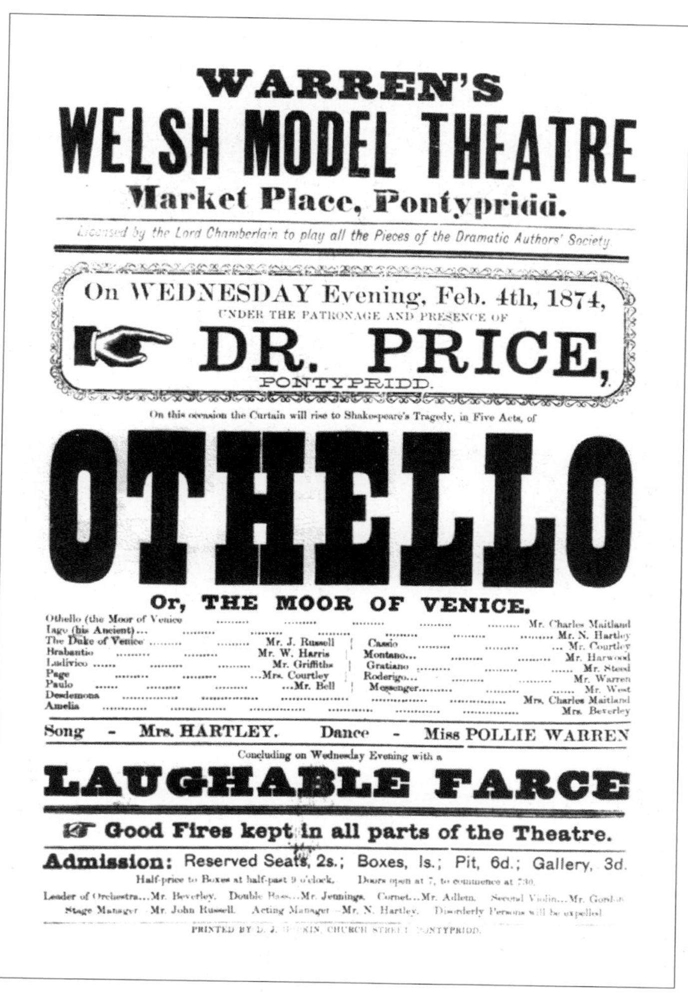

Above: A poster advertising a performance of Shakespeare's *Othello* at Market Square, February 1874. The play was performed under the auspices of none other than Dr William Price who was known for his support of several philanthropic events throughout the market town.

Opposite above: Congregational singing at Ynysangharad War Memorial Park.

Opposite below: Drummer Chris Slade (Christopher Rees) with Elvis Presley and Tom Jones. Born in Belle Vue, Treforest in October 1946 Chris was an original member of Tom's band The Senators. In 1958, he won a scholarship to Pontypridd Grammar School and it was there that he took up drumming and he actually played on the original demo of Tom's first hit single, *It's Not Unusual*. He subsequently toured with Tom before departing in 1969 to join the group called 'Tomorrow' featuring a young Olivia Newton-John. Chris later joined Manfred Mann's Earth Band in March 1972, remaining with them for six years. He went on to play with Paul Rodgers (of Free and Bad Company fame) in The Firm and also with Pink Floyd's David Gilmour. He probably received his highest exposure in 1989 when he was asked to join AC/DC. He later worked with Jimmy Page and Gary Newman before launching a new band called Asia before departing in 2005 and working on a new album with British power trio Damage Control.

Gwyn Davies of Thompson Street, Hopkinstown, projectionist and manager for decades of the Regent Cinema with Pontypridd Urban District Council chairman Cllr George Paget, when two new projectors were installed in 1932.

Mona Gray, manageress of the White Palace Cinema, Pontypridd, December 1984. Then aged ninety, she had worked behind the sweet counter or as manageress since a young woman and was recognised as the oldest cinema manageress in the country. Sadly the White Palace was demolished in 1991 with the rest of the street in an effort to create an inner-relief road which aimed to free Pontypridd from further traffic congestion.

Argraffiad Coffadwriaethol

Commemorative Copy of the

O'r Don Byd Adnabyddus

World-famed Hymn-tune

Cwm Rhondda

GYFANSODDWYD GAN
Y DIWEDDAR

Composed by the late

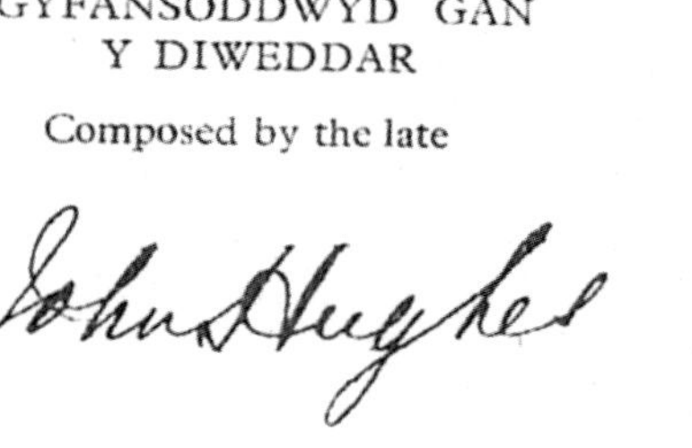

Hymn writer John Hughes (1873-1932) who composed the hymn tune *Cwm Rhondda*. Born in Dowlais before moving to Tonteg as a baby, composer John Hughes began his working life at the age of twelve as a door boy in a coal mine in Llantwit Fardre before becoming a clerk at the Great Western Colliery in Pontypridd. He was a deacon and precentor at Salem Baptist chapel and in 1907 was invited to write a tune for a music festival at Capel Rhondda, Hopkinstown which coincided with the installation of a new pipe organ. Taking the set of words written by hymn writer William Williams (Pantycelyn) called *Arglwydd Arwain Trwy'r Anialiwch* and translated by Peter Williams into the more recognisable *Guide Me, O Thou Great Jehovah*, he set about his task and composed probably the most famous Welsh hymn tune ever written. The hymn describes the Biblical story from the book of Exodus of the Israelites travelling through barren lands while escaping slavery in Egypt before arriving in the land of Canaan. Performed on 1 November 1907 with John Hughes playing the mighty organ, it was originally called *Rhondda* in honour of the chapel but under the advice of conductor Harry Evans was renamed *Cwm Rhondda* in 1908 so it wouldn't be confused with another hymn of the same name by Treherbert composer M.O. Jones. Within a few short years its appeal spread far and wide enjoying growing international appeal in both a religious and sporting setting which somewhat upset the Baptist movement who were infuriated that it was performed 'at football matches and on charabanc trips'. It was performed by the Royal Welch Fusiliers as they went into the slaughter at Mametz Wood on the Somme and in June 1918 featured in an evensong service in Westminster Abbey attended by Her Majesty Queen Mary and David Lloyd George who wrote letters of congratulations to the composer. He was invited to conduct a trio of major public performances in Cardiff, Newport and Pontypridd for audiences of 30,000 people or more and it became a popular addition to the congregational singing in sporting events and eisteddfodau. On 18 May 1927 John Hughes conducted a choir of a dozen miners for a live radio broadcast at the bottom of Pwllgwaun Colliery and accepted the invitation to conduct the hymn at a series of high-profile music festivals in Cardiff, Newport and Pontypridd. At the 1928 Treorchy National Eisteddfod its impromptu performance by 20,000 spectators including Prime Minister Stanley Baldwin, halted the unpleasant heckling of Communist Party members in the main marquee. Following a short illness John Hughes died at Tregarth on 14 May 1932 as *Cwm Rhondda's* popularity continued to increase. It was later sung in the Hollywood films *How Green Was My Valley* and *The African Queen* and was performed at the funeral of Diana, Princess of Wales and Queen Elizabeth the Queen Mother.

Sunken Gardens, Ynysangharad War Memorial Park. Ynysangharad Fields were acquired by the PUDC in 1919 and opened as a park in memory of those who made the ultimate sacrifice on 6 August 1923 by Field Marshall Lord Allenby. Grand memorial gates of iron, which are no longer there, stood at the main entrance of the park in Bridge Street. The park gleamed like a jewel in the town for people seeking sports activities, rest and relaxation, or walks in the spacious greenery.

Opening of the swimming pool in Ynysangharad War Memorial Park, 1927. On 30 July Dr D.G. Hughes, the chairman of Pontypridd Urban District Council and Cllr William Jones, chairman of the parks committee, officially opened the new swimming pool – better known as 'Ponty Baths'.

Swimming baths at Ynysangharad Park. Around 600,000 gallons of water was pumped through the purification plan each twenty-four hours, with Ynysangharad reputed to be the largest open-air swimming pool in Wales. It was here that great swimmers like Jenny James and Roy Hunt learned their craft. Although now in a sorry state, the lido is in fact a Grade II Listed Building.

A statue to Evan and James James at Ynsyangharad Park. Schoolmaster Rhys Morgan initiated a memorial fund to honour the composers. On 23 July 1930, Lord Treowen, watched by some 10,000 people, unveiled the memorial in Ynysangharad Park. Designed by Sir William Goscombe John, it consists of two bronze figures. They are a woman representing poetry and a male harpist representing music, and is set on a plinth of blue pennant stone from Craig-yr-Hesg quarry.

Ynysangharad War Memorial Park. The park was laid out on a triangular area of land between Ynysangharad House and the Brown Lenox chainworks and made up of fields, allotment gardens and an orchard. In 1893 a huge pavilion had been erected on the site for the National Eisteddfod of that year. In 1919 thirty-three acres of the site was bought 'for providing enjoyment and pleasure

for it inhabitants'. The original ideas for the layout of the park was for a formal design of tree-lined walks around various sports facilities, but when it was laid out a less formal approach was used with the major sporting facilities located at the southern end of the park.

Boxer Frank Moody. Born in Pontypridd in 1900, Frank was known affectionately as the 'Pontypridd Puncher' and from the age of eleven was working in the pits until his boxing success turned him professional in the 1920s. He knocked out Tommy Milligan in fifty-eight seconds in Glasgow in 1928 and beat everyone in Wales near his weight. Frank earned titles as British middleweight and light heavyweight champion. In 1918 he became light heavyweight champion of Great Britain. During his career he fought Hall of Famers, Ted 'Kid' Lewis, Harry Geb, Tiger Flowers and Maxie Rosenbloom. Frank's most impressive win came against Kid Norfolk when he knocked him out in the fourth round. His brother Glen was also a successful fighter. His first fight was an exhibition bout held to raise money to feed hungry children during the miners' strike of 1926. He later became Welsh middleweight and light heavyweight champion.

Pontypridd Chainworks Crusaders Football Club, winners of the Glamorgan Times Challenge Cup and Gold Medals, Season 1895-1896. Pictured back row, left to right: W. Whitehead, J. Walsh, J. Lifield, T. Allen (treasurer), T. Thomas (vice-president), J. Casey, W. Stockden, W. Angurn. Middle row: T. Harry (touch judge), T. Morris, I. Caple, W. Wilkins (captain), L.l. Whitehead (vice-captain), J.R. Jones, A. Jones, Tom Phillips (secretary), J. Coslett, I. Wilkins, E. Morgan, D. Morgan.

Pontypridd Golf Links. The golf club was formed in 1905 after a group of local businessmen met in the billiard room of the Gelliwastad Institute. A local solicitor, Mr J. Colenso Jones, proposed that a survey should be made to find a site suitable for a course. It was found above the Common, a tract of land some 400ft above sea level. At a meeting in the Park Hotel, Pontypridd, the Pontypridd Golf Club was formed, with Mr Owen Thomas as secretary, a position he held for forty years. Clubs and balls were produced, some of the undergrowth was cleared and two holes were made playable. By the end of the first year, the new club had enrolled ninety-one members. Fees were a guinea for gentlemen and half a guinea for ladies (of which the club had twenty-eight members). In 1907 Edwin Bradbeer of Burnham, was appointed as golf course planner. The first club captain (1905-06) was T. R. Griffiths, and one of his main tasks was to decide on the proposed idea for a new club house. Plans were prepared, and the new pavilion was ready for use in 1909.

Unfortunately, disaster struck just before the opening ceremony – the building was destroyed by fire. Fortunately, the building was insured the new pavilion was opened in 1910. There was no steward, but a 'cleaner' under the supervision of Miss Ethel Jones. After the First World War progress was resumed and by 1921, the club had 300 members and eighteen holes, the last five new ones overlooking the Treforest district along the Graig-yr Helfa Road. In 1926, the clubhouse was extended to incorporate living quarters for the new steward and his wife but twenty years later a disastrous fire completely destroyed the club house and all its equipment. Nothing daunted the members and within a year brick house was completed. By 1948, the club had its third pavilion, and a membership of 300. In 1961, another new clubhouse was built, alongside the existing one followed by the most recent stone-built headquarters in 1979.

Pontypridd Football Club, 1892–1893. Back row, left to right: Ben Lewis, Alun Morgan, Tom Murray. Middle row: Jack Murray, Patsy Devereaux, Harry Williams, Ack Llewellyn, Harry Stead, Tom Hemsworth, A.B. Evans. Front row: Jack Wilkins, Billy Gay, Jimmy Green, Jimmy Lewis, Billy Parkin and Tom Bryant.

Opposite above: Pontypridd Cricket Club, 1909. The club was formed in May 1870 and played its first match, against the Publicans Eleven, in the grounds of Gelliwastad House. Pontypridd had a strong and stylish cricket team in 1897 when the Glamorgan Cricket League was established. In the 1896 season the club was undefeated in the league and won the league championship. The club moved to Ynysangharad Park in 1924. Some seasons later, the club affiliated to the Glamorgan County Cricket Club, who had paid half the £800 cost of a new pavilion, and the first county match was played in the park, with Derbyshire the opponents.

Opposite below: Pontypridd Cricket Club 1st XI, 1937. Back row, left to right: B. Hughes (chairman), L. Williams (umpire), B. Williams, T. Reblin, G. Wride, L. Morgan, W. Norris, R. Evans. J. Harrison (scorer), R.R. Jenkins, F. Fawson (secretary), H. Edwards (groundsman). Middle row: B. Lewis, E.F. Lewis (vice captain), E. Mort (captain). K. Wride, W. Davies. Front row: T. Jenkins, R. Hendy.

Pontypridd Schools Cricket League, Winners of the Western Mail Shield, 1939. Back row, left to right: Committee members D. Herbert, T.J. Davies, W.G. Morgan (treasurer), D. Haydn Jones (secretary), T.E. Thomas, E.F. Lewis, W.J.A. Evans. T.H. Archer, D.R. Chubb, E.J. Felix (vice chairman), J. Protheroe (chairman). Third row: D. Volk, K. Fowler, E. Davies. Second row: J.A. Davies, R. Davies, F. Davies. Des Jones (captain), G. Mordecai, E. Wallace, W.J. Prosser. Front row: J. Harris, Alun Jones.

Pontypridd Cricket Club, 1940. Top row, left to right: B. Hughes, H. Edwards, S. Jones, B. Lewis, J. Harrison (scorer), H. Owen, W. Evans (secretary) T. Phillips, L. Parker. Front row: A. Jenkins, B. Lewis (vice captain), E.F. Lewis (captain), T. Jenkins, W.J. Hyett.

Pontypridd Cricket Club, 1952/53/54. Back row, left to right: G. Hendy, H. Wallace, W.J. Hyett. Middle row: R. Morgan, J.W. Griffiths (chairman), H. Woods, K. James, F. Fowler, K. Fowler, R. Morris, J. Rowlands, W.W.R. Hawkins (secretary), W.O. Robotham. Front row: R. Jones, W. Hoskin, H. Morgan (captain), Police Supt A. Morris (president), J. Smith (vice captain), K. Wride, R. Davies. I. Joseph.

Cricketer Bernard Hedges. Born in Pontypridd in November 1927 his sporting life began as a rugby player with Pontypridd and Swansea and was even selected to play in a final Welsh trial. But it was cricket in which he excelled and played for Glamorgan between 1950 and 1967, becoming known for his outstanding play as a right-handed batsman. During this time he amassed over 17,000 runs in first class cricket and in 1963 scored the county's first ever 100 in one-day cricket with 103 against Somerset in their Gillette Cup match at the Arms Park. The batsman joined Glamorgan after completing his National Service and initially played in the middle-order. He moved up to open the batting in the late 1950s and his sound technique and steadfast temperament allowed him to become a successful opening batsman. He was also a fine player of spin bowling and displayed nimble footwork against slow bowlers. One of his finest innings was the 139 made against Nottinghamshire on a turning wicket at Stradey Park, Llanelli when he mastered the wiles of Australian leg-spinner Bruce Dooland.

James Edward Spickett was born in Pontypridd in 1859. He was the eldest of two sons born to Edward Colnett Spickett. He became the registrar of Pontypridd, a post he inherited on his father's death in 1899 and held for forty-two years. As James and his brother William grew up, they were sent to Monkton House School, Cardiff, where they learned to play rugby in the school team. James left school first and became an articled clerk with his father's firm, Spickett & Co., Solicitors, in Courthouse Street. He decided to form a team of his own and with help from his brother and the chief clerk, Walter Morgan, he recruited other junior clerks at the Pontypridd County Courthouse and other middle-class youths of the town to play in his team. He arranged an inaugural meeting in 1878 at the Butcher's Arms Hotel. At the age of seventeen, he became the first captain of a club named after the town – Pontypridd. James's playing career was not long, although he and his brother did appear for the South Wales Football Club in representative matches – a precursor of provincial rugby. He passed his final law examination with first class honours in 1882 and was listed fifth in Britain. He entered the family legal firm, founded by his father in the 1860s, where he practised as a solicitor and JP for the next fifty years. He was the author of *The Handbook of County Court Practice*, featuring a collection of precedents of county court costs. James was a member of the first Pontypridd District Council, elected in 1894 to represent the Graig. In 1897 he was instrumental in founding *The Observer*, which was later transferred to the proprietorship of Percy Phillips. He was also one of the senior members of the Merlin Lodge of Freemasons and of the English Congregational church, Gelliwastad Road. On a more personal side, he was a keen footballer, photographer, fisherman, yachtsman and entomologist. He also devoted a lot of time to the volunteer movement, holding his first commission from Queen Victoria in the Submarine Miners and during the First World War, he organised the training of a company of volunteers, of which he was captain. At that time, in spite of increasing years, he insisted on taking a course of guards' training at Chelsea Barracks and elsewhere. Tributes were paid to him on his retirement as registrar of the Pontypridd, Ystrad, Caerphilly and Aberdare County Courts at Pontypridd County Court in July 1940. James and his father before him, had held the office of registrar for the greater part of 100 years. On Wednesday 2 September 1947, he arrived at the council offices at 6 p.m. for a meeting of the Burial Board. He did not feel well and went into the cloakroom. A member present at the meeting heard a thud. Cllr J. R. Clayton, an ambulance officer, who went to see what had happened, found Mr Spickett had collapsed. A doctor was summoned and James's daughter, Daisy was informed and soon arrived at the council chamber. Dr Arthur Jenkins, the family doctor, also came but, about half an hour later, Mr Spickett had passed away. He was eighty-seven years of age.

Opposite below: Pontypridd RFC XV 1947-1948 season. Back row, left to right: T. Woods, T. Hughes, D. Davies, V. Merry, W. Caldicott, T. Buckthought, F. Shallis, D. Love, H. Vaughan, T. Rowlards (referee). Front row: H. Leadbeter, D. Prater, L. Arnold (captain), E. Hitchens, D. Brewer, R. Gard, H. Alderman, L. Williams.

Right: Pontypridd rugby captain, Ernest George (1894-1895). He played for Wales against Scotland and Ireland in the 1894 to 1895 season. Pontypridd Rugby Football Club was formed in 1876, and was sufficiently well established by March 1880 to be one of nine clubs that met at the Tenby Hotel, Swansea, to discuss the formation of a national union. In 1886-87 the headquarters of the club was the Maltsers Arms and it played its home matches at Ynysangharad Fields. In 1890-91 the club moved to a field alongside the River Taff at Treforest, and began the development of the famous Taff Vale Park. The final Welsh trial was held there in December 1892. The club then moved to the People's Park in Mill Street in 1901, and it stayed there for three seasons. Then, on 1 October 1904, it played Caerphilly in the first game on a new pitch at Ynysangharad Fields. Although the club later returned to Taff Vale Park for a short time, it was back at Ynysangharad by 1908 and stayed there for sixty-six years before moving to the famous Sardis Road site.

Above: Pontypridd RFC XV, 1958-1959 Season. Back row, left to right: G. Gittins, B. Mapstone, D. Rogers, R. Jones, D. Harris, E. Jones, L. Davies, R. Rees. Middle row: J. Powell, S. Thomas, J. Watkins (captain), T. Ryan, J. Davies. Front row: T.B. Williams, W. Griffiths.

Below: Pontypridd RFC XV, 1968-1969 Season. Back row, left to right: G. Thomas, G. Rees, R. Jones, C. Owen, R. Pemberthy, C. Blacker, R. Hope, D. Edwards. Middle row from left: D. John, J. Smith, A. Jones (captain), T. David, R. Hope. Front row: M. Rivers, W. Evans.

Pontypridd RFC XV, 1982-1983 season. Back row, left to right: C. Morgan, M. Orsi, A. Sheppard, G. Jones, P. McBride, T. Bartless, M. Owen. Middle row: B. Hubbard, K. Trevett, B. Bolderson, N. Wilding, B. Fox, R. Pemberthy, G. Davies, R. Dyer, M. Owen, T. Anderson (trainer). Front row: A. Cartwright, S. Cannon, M. Alexander (captain), A. Witts, S. Smith.

Pontypridd Dragons football team. They were formed in Pontypridd in the summer of 1911 and played their first ever game against Queens Park Rangers in a friendly match at Taff Vale Park on 4 September 1911. The team featured several players who had played in the Football League but lost 2-1 in front of 4,000 spectators. Pontypridd competed in the second division of the Southern League from 1911, finishing fifth, seventh, eighth and eleventh before football was suspended in 1915 due to the First World War. When games recommenced from 1919, Pontypridd finished fourth twice in succession, fifth, fourth again, third in 1923/24 and 1924/25, but in 1925/26 finished last but one and folded in 1926 due to financial difficulties and the loss of the lease at Taff Vale Park. Among the many notable matches at Taff Vale Park was the visit of Aston Villa for a friendly on 20 April 1920 as part of the conditions in the transfer of H. Nash between the two teams. Villa won 5-3 but a week later the same line up beat Huddersfield 1-0 in the FA Cup Final! In March 1924 Tottenham Hotspur were the visitors for a match to commemorate the opening of Pontypridd's new 3,000 capacity stand.

Pontypridd, *c.* 1970. The author would like to record his thanks to the generous assistance of the staff of Pontypridd Library and their fine photographic archive department. A special thank you to librarians Hywel Matthews, Edwina Smart and Nick Kelland. Also for the support of Bryan Davies and staff at Pontypridd Museum, Steve Reardon at Pontypridd RFC, Andrew Hignell of Glamorgan Cricket Club, rugby historian Gareth Harris and transport historian Peter Gould. Special thanks must also go to historian D. J. Rees for allowing permission to reproduce his photographs and also to the author's late uncle Don Powell for his massive contribution to recording the history of the town.

Other local titles published by Tempus

Pontypridd A Market Town

DEAN POWELL

Compiled with 200 images, this selection highlights some of the changes and events that have taken place in the South Wales market town of Pontypridd. From glimpses of heavy industry, including the Ynysangharad Works and surrounding collieries, to the arrival of the first electric tram to Pontypridd in March 1905, all aspects of working and social life are chronicled here. Aspects of everyday life are also recalled, from shops and pubs, places of worship and public buildings, to celebrations and local sporting heroes.

978 07524 3578 7

Llantrisant Revisited

DEAN POWELL

This fascinating collection of over 200 old images pays tribute to the people who have proudly called Llantrisant their home. Commanding an outstanding setting on the crest of a hill, Llantrisant's splendour lies in its enchanting beauty and celebrated past. Bloodthirsty battles, pioneering acts of cremation and captured kings of England have all played a part in shaping the town, as have the generations of families who have lived here.

978 07524 3216 X

Upper Rhondda The Third Selection

EMRYS JENKINS AND ROY GREEN

This third fascinating collection of archive photographs of Upper Rhondda traces some of the many ways in which the region changed during the 1970s and 1980s. All aspects of everyday life are recorded, from shops and businesses, churches and schools, to images of work and leisure, day trips and days off. Its landscapes and landmarks are captured in this valuable historical record of life in the Upper Rhondda as it used to be and the changes that have since taken place.

978 07524 0366 4

Cilfynydd

DEAN POWELL

This absorbing collection of archive images provides a comprehensive glimpse into the history of Cilfynydd during the last 120 years. Compiled with over 200 images, this selection highlights the history of this industrial Welsh village, one that would witness one of the worst colliery disasters in mining history, only to be further decimated by an incredible tornado some years later. The book will delight and will evoke memories of a bygone time for those who have lived here.

978 07524 3780 1